Losing
YOUR LUGGAGE

Losing YOUR LUGGAGE

10 Pieces of Church Baggage
We All Need to Drop

GREGORY KLINE

LOSING YOUR LUGGAGE
Copyright © 2014 by Greg Kline

Scripture quotations are taken from the Holman Christian Standard Bible®, Copyright © 1999, 2000, 2002, 2003, 2009 by Holman Bible Publishers. Used by permission.

Printed in Canada

ISBN: 978-1-4866-0723-5

Word Alive Press
131 Cordite Road, Winnipeg, MB R3W 1S1
www.wordalivepress.ca

Library and Archives Canada Cataloguing in Publication

Kline, Gregory, 1971-, author
       Losing your luggage : 10 pieces of church baggage we all need to drop / Gregory Kline.

Issued in print and electronic formats.
ISBN 978-1-4866-0723-5 (pbk.).--ISBN 978-1-4866-0724-2 (pdf).--
ISBN 978-1-4866-0725-9 (html).--ISBN 978-1-4866-0726-6 (epub)

       1. Christian life. I. Title.

BV4501.3.K547 2014   248.4   C2014-906199-4
                                              C2014-906200-1

Dedication

This book is dedicated to Shannon, the love of my life, who continually encourages me to surrender and become the man God wants. Also, my parents, Bob and Linda, who modelled for me what it means to love God in every part of one's life. I also want to acknowledge every person in the church who, through patience and self-sacrifice, has built into my life a godly heritage which cannot be lost.

Contents

Preface

Medical school ruined my ability to read.

For nine years, I read nothing except scientific papers and medical textbooks. A well-written scientific text is completely devoid of emotion or colour. No opinions, no allegory, no stories, no plot, no suspense, no beautiful words, no reflection. Just a series of facts, connected by words that are basically inconsequential beyond their ability to place those facts in an English sentence. I learned to read these books speedily, fifty pages per night, ignoring anything that wasn't a fact, pausing only momentarily to mentally insert a new fact into a cognitive algorithm, and then checking off a tick box in my mind. *Check, new fact installed.*

After so many years, this type of third-person, emotionless reading became the only type of literature I even wanted to read. My wife Shannon still tells stories of how I brought a small but thick medical textbook on our first vacation after we were married. I distinctly remember sitting on a beach towel in front of a beautiful lake on a hot summer day... reading about the use of a certain diagnostic test for pulmonary embolism detection. The thought of reading a novel or any work of fiction seemed absolutely ludicrous, a complete waste of time. Who would ever read a made-up story when you could be spending that time cramming more facts into your memory?

This way of reading even rolled over into the way I read my Bible. I could read multiple chapters relatively quickly, my mind searching for new "facts" which I could commit to memory—names and features of biblical characters, sequences of events, locations of certain passages, and text summaries that supported certain ethical positions. No interactions with the text, just cognitive processing. All of it, as fast as possible—and very dry, as you might imagine.

Then, one day, everything changed. We were on another vacation (believe me, I do work in between these vacations) and I must have finished reading the medical papers I'd brought along because I somehow found myself staying at a beach resort with nothing to read. So we visited a little bookshop which, to my horror, contained nothing but novels. Shannon basically forced me to buy one—*To Kill a Mockingbird*, which I hadn't read in school as a boy.

It was a revelation. I found myself in awe of the story, moved by the characters, rooting for Atticus as he fought community prejudice all by himself. I didn't want it to end. I learned how to interact with words again.

Since then, I still read medical papers out of duty and I feel most comfortable with a nonfiction book, but my novel reading has increased. I now relish starting to read something by well-regarded novelists both old and new. *A Tale of Two Cities* is probably my all-time favourite, Victorian verbosity and all.

Don't be like me in medical school.

Please don't read this book like some kind of scientific text. I didn't write it using a dispassionate third-person approach. I interacted with the words as they appeared on the screen. I actually prayed the prayers as I wrote them. I imagined having a conversation about the text with my closest friends and family. And that's what this book is: a conversation. A conversation with myself, and with you—with God invited to speak as well, wherever He wills.

I encourage you to read slowly. I assure you, I wrote it slowly! There's nothing in here to be memorized and there isn't going to be a test at the end. Feel free to argue with me as you read. Argue with yourself even! But by the end of the book, if this has started a conversation between you and God, I will be happy. And if these words can be of any use in leading to a fuller surrender to God's work in you, I will be positively ecstatic. Thanks for reading!

Introduction

Thank goodness for the church library. Last week, my family and I arrived early on Sunday morning because Shannon had to set up her Sunday School class. As much as I love our church, and I do love our church, I'm not excited about showing up at 9:30 a.m. when the service doesn't start until 10:15. Except for the pastor and worship band in the main sanctuary, if you show up at 9:30, you'll be the only person there. Since the kids run off to the gym, that leaves me alone, basically rocking on my heels, slack-jawed, and staring at the missionary board display which hasn't changed since 2010. Yup, McDougalls are still in Togo. Keep praying they get that car fixed; it apparently broke down in late 2009.

Then, once the people start trickling in, it sometimes feels even more awkward. The first people to arrive are the coffee bar folks, who get right to work, and then the greeters, who are mostly there to greet people who arrive at the right time, not the inexplicably early foyer-loiterers like me. At that point, I usually head over to the info desk and pretend to be intently interested in the application brochure for our local Christian College. I stare at it for about ten minutes until I become super conscious of the fact that no one is going to mistake me for a high school senior. That's when the library opens and becomes a safe haven to hang out—until there's enough people I know to bring me back out to socialize. Should I be better at just introducing myself to people and chatting up whoever's there? Probably, but on some Sundays that's just not in my comfort zone, so the library often ends up winning my attention for a few minutes.

Having said that, the church library is no corner behind the stairs. I really do like being in there. So many books, so many topics. I'll often read a chapter or two before making a mental note to put a particular title on my future reading list. The problem is that my list of books to read has long since become completely unwieldy, to the point where I'll need to become a full-time monk just to have any hope of reading it all. My kids love to point out that my hairline has already become like that of a medieval monk, so maybe it would be a good fit.

All joking aside, I rarely allow myself to take any library books home. The reason is that if I do, I'm probably going to try to read them. Crazy, eh? But here's the thing: taking books home means I'm going to have to put all other reading aside, particularly my Bible.

Now, I love the Bible. Or perhaps it would be more honest to say that I want to love the Bible. However, a sad truth about me is that I'm easily drawn to books *about* the Bible, which I'll often choose to read instead of the Bible. A book that traces the historical character of Paul and how it influenced his style of writing? Yes! The letter to the Galatians? Uh, sure. A book that examines the biblical arguments for various paradigms of God's gift of free will? Absolutely! The Proverbs? Okay, but not if I'm feeling really tired. Just being honest here.

And yet before you put down this book because of the spiritual failings of its author, I'm happy to report that God has slowly been giving me more and more desire to be in His Word, interacting with Him. The ancillary books I so eagerly read are not entirely without value, and in many cases they have greatly enhanced my love for a God who has somehow been able to convey, in the writing of one book, everything we need to know to live with Him each day. As such, I want to learn to love that book even more and treat its text with the utmost care in any writing I produce.

This brings me to my first personal objection to writing any books at all: I don't want to write a book that takes up space in a good church library, and I certainly don't want to add to the literary distractions that take people away from reading God's Word. So if you plan on reading this book (and aren't just reading the introduction to escape an uncomfortable conversation in the church foyer), please, please do me the favour of making sure you spend as much time in the Word as you do in this book.[1]

---

1 For those needing a place to start, my personal favourite books are Matthew and Luke, as you'll likely notice later on.

This brings me to problem number two. I certainly cannot claim to be a formally trained biblical scholar. I'm not a pastor. I didn't go to Bible school. I don't make any claims to "special revelation." I could never give lectures on biblical exposition techniques. As it is, I'm going to need to have a couple of seminary graduates look this over to make sure I haven't gone off the theological rails.

So by what authority do I write this book? Let me be clear: I'm not claiming any special authority. However, I just might be an expert at churchgoing, along with the thinking and attitudes that are acquired in the process. A well-known book now claims that it takes ten thousand hours of practice to become an expert on a subject. Well, if I consider my conscious life as starting from age five, that gives me thirty-eight years of attending church. Since each Sunday is probably a three-hour commitment, at fifty weeks a year (no church on vacation), that makes 150 hours per year, totalling 5,700. Add in the weekly hours from junior high and high school youth group, then college and career, and it probably sits at seven thousand hours. Then I have six full summers of Christian camping, fifteen years of small groups, and all the retreats, special speakers, vacation Bible schools, men's breakfasts, and Wednesday night adult study classes. I was in a Christian men's quartet for three years.[2] Add in five years as a youth sponsor, three years as worship band leader, five short-term mission trips, and a stint on the board of elders, and all together it probably sums up to just over ten thousand hours. And I didn't even include those old-school Sunday night church services from way back in the day—and those hymns with seven verses each, and you sing every single one along with the chorus every time so it seems to take a whole hour. Thus, I feel quite confident in claiming to be an expert in being "churched."

Teasing aside, the church, when it works as it should, is a beautiful thing. This book is the culmination of lessons I've learned from reading, from conversations with fellow Christians who have earned respect for their wisdom, from my own self-reflection, and hopefully from things

---

2 Hey, we were good and we were cool. I prefer to remember it more as a Christian "boy band." My wife's not so sure…

God has pointed out along the way as I strive to "be like Jesus," as my pastor likes to say.

As a teacher, at the start of any lecture preparation I always ask myself, "What do I hope the people do with the information and presentation I'm about to make?" I ask myself the same question of this book. I've observed in my own heart that there are really only three useful and meaningful responses to biblical teaching: a greater love or awe of God, confession/repentance of one's failures, and a renewed commitment to the surrender of my life to Him. May God use my experiences and thoughts to challenge you to examine your own life, to respond in one of these three meaningful ways, and to drop any remaining "church baggage" that's holding you back!

For those who are only reading because the line-up at the church foyer coffee bar is still too long… don't worry, I'm not offended. I'd stay in the library, too.

Where Did All That
Luggage Come From?

I 'll never forget traveling as a family when our kids were really little. Our extended family is spread across North America, and each year we tried to meet for a week in North Carolina. It was always a glorious week in the sun, but getting there was usually a disaster. We'd take three suitcases— one for our clothes, one for the kids' clothes, and one full of diapers. Also, a portable playpen, my golf clubs, and four backpacks full of plastic toys, crayons, and stickers to keep the kids busy. Oh yes, and a portable plastic toilet. Nothing like wheeling a cart loaded with suitcases through the airport, topped by a bright blue and white toilet!

The kids weren't too happy about the hassle of travel, either. At the end of a long flight once, we just sat on the runway, waiting to disembark. It was hot, we were tired, and we felt hemmed in by our backpacks, bags, pillows, and jackets. Our youngest daughter, who was about three, had had enough. With a grouchy look on her face, she yelled out, "I want some lipstick!" (meaning chap stick), to which we heard some other passenger reply, "You got that right, sister!" My wife had to then rummage through all the baggage to find the elusive chap stick before things really got out of hand.

Where does all that luggage come from? We have a special room for it in our house: a long, unfinished closet under the basement stairs. Some of it is old, like the teal green cloth folding suit cover with the faux leather corners I got in the early 90s. Haven't used it for twenty years, but for some reason we choose to keep it. Then there's the newer luggage—that huge blue suitcase we bought for a Europe trip only to discover that when it's full, it weighs three hundred pounds. All in all, I bet we have fifteen pieces of baggage, just sitting there. We even moved it all—empty—from our old house to our new house. Just so we could keep it, I guess. I'd sure hate to lose that stretchy red bag that still smells like the inside of rotten sea shells from our Florida trip.

Luggage. Such a good word for it. With bags like ours, packed full of all the stuff we don't seem to be able to travel without, there's no such thing as "carrying" or "portering" the bags. You lug 'em. And of course, when we travel, I'm way too cheap to hire a taxi into town from the airport. Not when there's a subway line you can ride for two dollars.

And so we lug. Up and down the stairs of the subway, through the transfer stations, dragging them along the floors of subway cars and lifting them up over turnstiles. Along the sidewalks, usually uneven cobblestone, and up three flights of stairs at the hotel. Of course, by the time I've lugged the luggage into the hotel room, I'm sweating profusely, my back is killing me, and my arms are numb from all the lifting.

The real travel pros often travel without suitcases, since they learn to do without the things everyone else seems to need. They'll tell you that luggage—or baggage, if you prefer—is only needed if you insist on bringing along your comfort items (or kids' plastic toys). The truth is, it weighs you down, slows your progress, and these days costs you money!

In many ways, it's the perfect metaphor for the "stuff" we collect and carry with us in our hearts and minds as we go along our spiritual journeys. It might be an attitude, a way of thinking, a particular understanding or misunderstanding of some principle, or even just a stereotyped reaction to a problem. In each case, our ways of thinking become comfortable, familiar, easy. But if we're incorrect in our understanding, the subsequent errors accumulate and can ultimately slow us down and tire us out.

Now, who needs some lipstick?

Where do we get our Christian luggage? I'm not entirely sure; I've never read a study or seen an authoritative list of sources, but my observations tell me that most of us who live in Christian circles long enough accumulate some degree of it over the years. In some cases, unfortunately, erroneous doctrines have been explicitly taught to us by well-intentioned church members and book authors. In other cases, our misunderstandings have arisen through words or the actions of others who implied certain beliefs or conclusions.

Since the first printing of the Bible, there has been debate whether the average, untrained believer can accurately understand and interpret Scripture on their own. While I firmly believe that every Jesus follower should own—and read—their own Bible, if you've been in the church long enough, you've probably heard someone talk about a scripture and what it means to them, which can occasionally be a very creative meaning, indeed. Even sincere, biblically trained believers can disagree on the proper interpretation of passages. How else could the church have ended up with thousands of denominations, each of which thinks they have it right?

This book is not intended to address the controversial passages that define denominations—for example, the style of baptism, arrangement of authority, the role of women, etc. For those who want further discussion of these perennially controversial areas, plenty of scholarly resources are available. Good luck, and if you figure out the "right" answer, do let me know.

The luggage I want to deal with in this book has little or nothing to do with biblical controversy. Rather, I want to delve into the personal effects of certain ideas and attitudes that have arisen in the culture of the Western church. Again, plenty of books do a masterful job of critiquing the Christianity culture of North America in particular, but my study is not interested in politics or large-scale culture; it's meant to be an examination of our individual hearts, which have been trained up in a shared church culture that transcends most denominations.

At this point, some readers may be getting ready to go on the defensive, thinking this is going to be a big, long critique of the church. After all, haven't many good people given their lives to the church and its work? Hasn't the church of modern times begun to rediscover its God-given mission to love and reach out to human brokenness all across the globe? Hasn't the church begun to evolve into a life-giving entity that welcomes outsiders rather than pushes them away? In many places, thankfully, the answer to those questions is a yes. How then can I begin to claim that our shared church culture sometimes unwittingly adds baggage to our spiritual lives?

The answer is that the church, beautiful as she is, is made up of not-yet-perfect people, myself most definitely included. As such, we are endlessly attracted to rules of thumb, laws of apparent cause-and-effect, formulas for "how to do it," and an ever-present thirst for new ideas to "do it better." The consequence is that we often filter God's word through this cultural sieve and end up with conclusions that fit with what we think should be true—for instance, that there should be easily applied, simple, and distilled principles of right and wrong for all situations, or that there should be clear spiritual duties, and often a particular focus on our personal contributions to God's work. These assumptions and understandings are passed consciously and unconsciously between Christians through all the different forms of our interactions within the church.

Thus far, this writing has been semiautobiographical, for indeed I am one who would like to believe that more knowledge, better critical thought, and an organized scriptural mind will result in automatic, Christ-like transformation. But over time, I've come to realize that some of this knowledge—misinterpreted, misapplied, and mixed in with our cultural traditions—is just baggage that gets in the way of the real (and only) way of becoming the people God wants us to be: knowing Jesus and surrendering one's life to the transformation He brings.

And so I have absolutely no interest in causing offense or being ungrateful for the spiritual heritage I've been given through the dedication of others who have supported and shaped me growing up in the church. The examples of many who have gone before us will always stand as a testimony to "salt and light" in our world. But I invite you now to hold fast to the godly spiritual legacy of the past, upon which we can build once more after we get rid of some of the comfortable and familiar baggage that weighs us down.

No more *lug*gage.

Luggage One

"If I really give my life to God, He'll make me go be a missionary in a jungle somewhere."

H ere's a confession from growing up in the church: I never liked "Mission Focus Weekends."

How's that for an awkward start to the book? Didn't I just say I didn't want to offend anyone? Don't get me wrong: I'm not saying I don't like missionaries. In fact, if I think of the most-respected Christians I know, quite a few are long-term missionaries.

As a child and teenager in the church, I didn't like going to services where some furloughed missionary spoke. Before the evening message, there would be a potluck dinner of sorts, featuring foods from the mission country (which always looked disgusting at age fourteen). Often, the stories were amazing—they lived in huts! had no contact with the outside world! frequently their kids had to live in a different country in order to go to school! Sometimes, there was an accompanying movie. Not a DVD, though, or even a VHS tape. An actual thirty-five-millimetre movie. Grainy film, lots of posed shots of people "helping," and the people receiving the help always nodded and smiled. The soundtrack was usually something that sounded like the background music from *Charlie's Angels*—or at least what it might sound like if played in a tin can.

Inevitably, the speaker would conclude by making a plea for others to come join the mission, quoting Matthew 9:37: *"The harvest is abundant, but the workers are few."* To which, I thought to myself, *No wonder the workers are few; it sounds terrible.* Add to this the reverence with which missionaries were viewed, rightfully so, and you can probably see why I started to piece together the idea that serving God meant giving Him your life, and in turn He would ship you out to the farthest jungle right away.

In addition, some of you may remember hearing the "Count the Cost" sermons. This was always a favourite theme for youth retreats. Certainly, the principle—or at least the words—are biblical. In Luke 14, Jesus cautions the crowds that are following Him, *"For which of you, wanting to build a tower, doesn't first sit down and calculate the cost to see if he has enough to complete it?"* (Luke 14:28) These are obviously logical and important words. In effect, He's telling the crowd that if they're just along for the entertainment of seeing miracles, they're missing the point of what it means to be His disciple. It was true then, and it's true now.

But in some sermons I've heard, it seems like the speaker has interpreted the words as a threat. This alternate, threatening version is perhaps best summarized in the beginning of Matthew Henry's commentary on the passage: "Those that undertake to follow Christ must count upon the worst and prepare accordingly."[3] In fairness, the full commentary on this passage does flush out a few reasonable details, but hopefully the reader can see that there are two very different sentiments here: Jesus' actual words, which caution His listeners to make Him the focus of their lives, versus the implication that doing so will certainly invite hardship and misery. Is it any wonder I always got a sickly feeling when faced with this veiled ultimatum? "If you want to follow Jesus, get ready to do everything you never wanted to do. For the rest of your life!"

And then there was Jonah. Jonah didn't want to go to Nineveh when God told him to, and how did that pan out? Sloshing around in some whale's mouth or belly for a couple days. I bet he didn't count that cost!

Do some believers experience hardship and misery? Certainly, and worse. Jesus always warned this would be a possibility— *"You will be hated by everyone because of My name"* (Matthew 10:22). However, this harsh expectation must be tempered with some of Jesus' other words, which follow just a few lines later:

> *Come to Me, all of you who are weary and burdened, and I will give you rest. All of you, take up My yoke and learn from Me, because I am gentle and humble in heart, and you will find rest for yourselves.* **For My yoke is easy and My burden is light.**
> Matthew 11:28–30 (emphasis added)

How can Jesus make these two apparently contradictory statements?

---

3 Matthew Henry. *Christian Classics Ethereal Library,* "Commentary on the Whole Bible Volume V." Accessed: August 17, 2014 (http://www.ccel.org/ccel/henry/mhc5.Luke.vi.html).

Hold that thought. First, let's ask a question: why do we so easily gravitate to the idea that fully surrendering our lives to God is tantamount to inviting ruin? Mull over that one for a while. This is something I've spent a long time considering. Maybe you've thought about it as well, and if you're like me, maybe you've dreamed up a whole bunch of horrible scenarios to test yourself. "Am I willing to get cancer for God? Am I willing to leave my family and go sleep in the homeless shelters for God? What if God wants me to quit my job and go hand out Bibles in the middle of a sniper war somewhere?" See, I can think of a whole bunch of situations that sound miserable, foolhardy, or both.

When thinking of such things, am I spiritually testing myself? Counting the cost? No. I've come to realize that such exercises are nothing more than indulgences to fear and selfishness. Fear that God doesn't have my best interests at heart, and selfishness for musing all the reasons that my plans for my life are the only ones that can produce happiness and satisfaction.

So how does it work for Jesus to reassure us that His burden is light, all the while reminding us that true followers must "give it all" to be disciples? I think the answer can be found in two passages about fish:

What man among you, if his son asks him for bread, will give him a stone? Or if he asks for a fish, will give him a snake? If you then, who are evil, know how to give good gifts to your children, how much more will your Father in heaven give good things to those who ask Him!
Matthew 7:9

"Follow Me," He told them, "and I will make you fish for people!"
Matthew 4:19

Did you catch it?[4] Jesus repeatedly reminds us that God is good. We think we know how to make our kids happy? Guess what, we know nothing compared to His knowledge and desire to give to us what is good. He's not up in heaven plotting some terrible disaster for us as soon as we give Him the go-ahead by surrendering our lives to Him. I understand that

---

4 Pun intended!

this statement opens the door to long conversations about why bad things happen, but putting that aside for now, regardless of some of the awful things that do happen in the world, Jesus reminds us that God's *desire* for our lives comes from His character (ultimate goodness) and His loving relationship with us (father/child).

The key part is *"I will make you fish for people."* He doesn't say, "I will call you and then send you out to do some stuff you're going to hate" or "I'll insinuate some stuff until you feel guilty enough to do it." Not even, "Go and figure out how to be a fisher of people."

Here's how these two verses come together to form one of the most beautiful and reassuring truths of discipleship. When we give our lives to Him, we can be confident in His goodness towards us such that He will transform us so we'll actually desire to do that which He has set aside for us. That's worth reading again! No fear. No threats. No guilt. No jungles—unless He transforms our hearts and gives us the burning desire to go there. For some, that's exactly what He does. For others, something else. Either way, it has nothing to do with fear of what He might ask. His yoke will be light, and following Him will be rest compared to the weariness of everything else.

The apostle Paul figured this out. Interesting thing about Paul; we sometimes put him on a pedestal, giving him such reverence that he appears to be the foremost spiritual giant of the New Testament writers. Yet Paul was still a man with admitted failings and weaknesses. We read about his shipwreck, his imprisonments and hardships, and assume it was all water off his back. I'm not so sure. Being shipwrecked would still be terrifying, even if you're trusting God to save you. Time in prison would be agonizing. Whippings hurt. In 2 Corinthians 1:8, Paul admits he was *"completely overwhelmed—beyond [his] strength—so that [he] even despaired of life."* I highly doubt Paul gave his life to Christ actively hoping for all these bad things to come his way. But look at his words to the Philippians: *"I am sure of this, that He who started a good work in you will carry it on to completion until the day of Christ Jesus"* (Philippians 1:6). Who starts the work? God. Who brings it to completion? God. And in the meantime? God changes our hearts, if we let Him, such that we actually desire the work He has set for us—work that's used by Him to build His Kingdom while bringing our Christ-like transformation to completion.

In writing to the Romans, Paul expressed his deep desire to come and minister to them (Romans 1:10). This letter was written during his third missionary journey. By that time, don't you think he was sick and tired of the traveling hassles, threats from the authorities, and the physical dangers involved? Yet it was his sincere wish for God to take him for even more such travel. How did he muster up that kind of desire for God's work? Go back to Philippians 1:6. It wasn't because Paul made himself into a spiritual giant; it was because God was bringing His work in Paul to its completion. Paul didn't lie awake dreading yet another missionary journey. At that stage, his transformed heart honestly, genuinely wanted to do it.

Let's get personal now. Unfortunately, I haven't yet come to the point of total submission in all areas like Paul did, but God is working on it. For several years, I had a gnawing feeling that God might be calling me to offer some service on the foreign medical mission field. In church, we sang songs with phrases like "I would go to the ends of the earth to tell Your story," and I wondered how I had the audacity to speak such words when they were probably untrue. In reality, I didn't want to go. It might be dangerous. I'd miss my family. The food would probably make me sick. I'm not a surgeon, just an endocrinologist, and nobody needs help with their testosterone levels "over there." After two or three years of feeling this call, I finally surrendered and filled out a medical service application with Samaritan's Purse. I remember the smug feeling I had after sending it in. "There you go, God, I did it. I surrendered. So now we can just put this behind us. They'll never need me. This was probably just a test to see if I would be willing to submit. Passed!"

Twenty-four hours later, the phone rang and Samaritan's Purse was calling to say they had just the place for me to go. Oh no.

It ended up being a difficult trip to Northeastern Ghana. Very hard work with very few resources. I've never seen so much tragedy in so little time, to the point where I think for a few months upon my return I was suffering from post-traumatic stress disorder. Not fun in the least, and the food *was* pretty bad—at least its effects upon me were pretty bad. However, through the experience, God changed my heart towards such missions. I'm now happy to submit every time God brings a similar opportunity my way, hence my return to Africa several times since. I'm no Christian hero.

I didn't attain some new spiritual plateau that allowed me to go; it was just pure and simple submission, after several years of fighting, with a resulting change of heart.

In retrospect, it truly amazes me. I went from a point of running away from God's leading to a point of actively asking God to send me out. I didn't talk myself into it, didn't read a persuasive argument, and didn't just convince myself it wouldn't be so bad. A moment of obedience led to God genuinely changing my heart.

Surrender of one's life without fear might be the toughest piece of baggage to drop. To be honest, this is one piece of baggage I tend to pick up repeatedly, so laying it down is a continuous process, not a one-time event. I need to surrender today and tomorrow and the day after that. And so on.

Each of these chapters will end with a prayer. I encourage you to read it over to get the general idea, then consider reading it again, this time as a prayer to God.

Heavenly Father,

You are my portion and my cup of blessing. You hold my future; the boundary lines have fallen for me in pleasant places. Indeed, I have a beautiful inheritance.

I will praise the Lord who counsels me. Even at night, my conscience instructs me. I keep the Lord in mind always. Because He's at my right hand, I will not be shaken (Psalm 16:5–8).

Thank You for Your goodness, which surpasses anything I can even imagine.

I don't have the courage within me to say yes to all the things that could possibly be asked of me. Even still, I surrender my will and life to Your purpose.

Complete in me the good work You have started, and in doing so release my grip on the "things" (and plans) I think I need.

Build into my heart a desire to do the work You have set for me, and may I learn to love You more all the while. Amen.

Luggage Two

"Riches are a spiritual hindrance."

But woe to you who are rich, for you have received your comfort.

Luke 6:24

But God said to him, "You fool! This very night your life is demanded of you. And the things you have prepared [earned]—whose will they be?"

Luke 12:20

Then Jesus said to His disciples, "I assure you: It will be hard for a rich person to enter the kingdom of heaven!"

Matthew 19:23

Come now, you rich people! Weep and wail over the miseries that are coming on you.

James 5:1

I once heard a good preacher say that he felt sorry for rich people, because they always get blasted in sermons and end up slinking out of the church with guilty looks on their faces. Without question, if you've grown up in the church, you've probably realized there's a very odd relationship between the church and its rich members.

On one hand, the rich tend to be very popular. As a kid, our church had a Christian family we'll call the Hughes. They had a mansion—a complete party house with indoor pool, billiards room, huge patio, trampoline, TV room, and even a VCR.[5] They used to open up their house for church events, and people flocked to it. Come early, leave late—the opposite of most Sunday mornings! We were all too happy to enjoy the shared riches of the Hughes. But how many times in church did we hear a call for donations and think to ourselves, *I hope the Hughes are listening!*

In many cases, the Hughes *were* listening. I've seen occasions when people like the Hughes are the only ones who really step up and contribute, sometimes with additional contributions at the last minute, to

---

5 Yup, this was the early 80s, folks.

balance the budget or fund the program. In some churches, this happens often enough that the self-defined "non-rich" might feel they can safely ignore financial requests because it's known that "the Hughes" will save the day. Even then, as we walk out to the church parking lot, we look judgmentally upon the Hughes' BMW X5 parked there. *Such bad stewardship,* we think to ourselves.

Thus far, I've used the term "we," but I should probably be more honest and use the term "I." I certainly tend to think that way.[6]

Before we really get into this, I want to be clear in laying the framework for the discussion. I don't intend to write about giving, tithing, financial stewardship, care of the poor, wealth as a blessing, or a global perspective on wealth. These are all important areas for study, and many useful books already provide excellent discussion of the biblical principles involved. Some of my favourites include Randy Alcorn's *The Treasure Principle,*[7] Ron Sider's *Rich Christians in an Age of Hunger,*[8] and *Hope Lives* by Amber Van Schooneveld.[9] As with all other chapters in this book, my focus is upon our attitudes towards the scripture we think we know, along with attitudes towards wealth and those in the church with wealth.

Let's start by defining "rich." In recent years, the media has created a definition for us by propagating terms like "the five percent," or even "the one percent," meaning the tiny percentage of people who control a disproportionately huge amount of a country's money and resources. When we hear that, I think we all immediately imagine some jet-set hedge fund manager or real-estate tycoon. The problem with this definition, of course, is that since very few of us achieve that kind of super-wealth, it puts the rest of us comfortably in the "not rich" category. That serves us well, since

---

6 More on this in the Luggage Ten section.

7 Randy Alcorn, *The Treasure Principle* (New York, NY: Random House, 2001).

8 Ron Sider, *Rich Christians in an Age of Hunger* (Downers Grove, IL: Intervarsity Press, 1977).

9 Amber Van Schooneveld, *Hope Lives* (Loveland, CO: Group Publishing, 2008).

it gives us the self-assurance that we don't need to be too worried about those troublesome "woe to the rich" passages in Scripture!

Before the media took care of this nasty, guilt-defining "rich" problem, I dare say most people would have defined "rich" according to visible possessions. Perhaps less consciously, the real definition would have been anybody who seemed to have more than you do! Interesting, isn't it? Virtually everybody would like to have more, if they're honest with themselves, yet no one in the church wants to be called rich. We love hearing the pastor rail away about greed and lack of generosity, especially since he's clearly sending a message to the Hughes over there! Preach it, brother!

Let's go a step further. Not only do we not want to be called rich, the sermon on the mount singles out the poor for special blessing. We might therefore assume that riches preclude any blessing. In our twisted thinking, the ideal might be for us to be rich enough to be comfortable in this life but poor enough to slide into that blessings category Jesus describes.

So, where exactly is that line?

I'd like to suggest that there are three functional categories of wealth in North America. First of all, there's the rich, and I've already talked about the media-driven definition of that. And of course there's the poor. But poor isn't just the opposite of rich. Virtually every authority who writes about poverty will tell you that it's not just the lack of finances that defines the condition. True poverty includes an aspect that's even worse than a lack of money—powerlessness, hopelessness, and/or oppression.

Among the people of Jesus' day, it might have been straightforward to differentiate the rich from the poor. The Jews were an oppressed nation, paying taxes to a foreign government, and it's probably fair to assume that most of the common folk had very little hope for imminent change or self-determination.

The poor are still present in every modern society, but what about the huge number of people today who are neither rich nor poor?

When I was a first-year medical resident in 1996, my total annual salary was $27,000. Was I rich? Definitely not by the standard we all use today. I couldn't afford a place to live besides a shared apartment. I had to lease my sensible car: a Mazda Protege. I took no interesting vacations, and I shopped at discount clothing stores. I owed a meaningful amount of each paycheque to the bank to repay my education loans. But was I poor? Absolutely not. I never experienced a feeling of hopelessness, never felt oppressed, and no matter how bad a day was, I knew I was working towards something better. The poor do not have the luxury of such confidence and hope. So if I wasn't rich and I wasn't poor, what would we call it? I suggest "non-rich."

It is probable that many or most people in North America today would identify with that third category. The only problem is, I'm not sure God sees it that way. I'm also not sure there are any differences in the attitudes seen in either the rich or non-rich.

Matthew 25:14–23 contains an interesting parable told by Jesus, commonly known as the parable of the talents. Notice that the first servant is given five talents (with one talent representing a Greek coin equivalent to six thousand days' wages), the second servant gets two talents, and the third servant gets one talent. As you may recall, the parable ends with the third servant being thrown out because he didn't invest the talent given to him and instead made some incorrect assumptions about the character of the Master. I think a lot of commentators have focussed on this third servant, the lesson being that we're expected to use the talents we have for God's greater glory. True enough. But if that's the only point, why did Jesus bother with the other part of the story, including the differing amounts given to the other servants? Why not just talk about the non-investing servant and his ultimate failure?

It's interesting to look at the first two servants. Clearly there was a discrepancy of wealth between them. One received an amount of money that would take eighty-two years to accumulate, the other had an amount representing thirty-three years of work. Sounds like the rich and the non-rich, by our present standards. But when each of those servants comes to give account of how they used their money, each has achieved an identical proportional increase. What does the Master (God) say to the first servant? *"Well done, good and faithful slave! You were faithful over a few things; I will put you in charge of many things. Share your master's joy!"* (Matthew 25:21) Then, what does the Master say to the second servant? *"Well done, good and faithful slave! You were faithful over a few things; I will put you in charge of many things. Share your master's joy!"* (Matthew 25:23) Notice that they heard the exact same thing, word for word. The Master told both servants that they were given "a few things," they had done well with what was given to them, and now they both got to enter the Master's joy.

Uh-oh. Looks like there's no difference in Jesus' view regarding the overall responsibility or reward for the rich and non-rich. Maybe our whole societal wealth spectrum and financial categorization reflects our own values more than God's.

So, if there isn't a clear line defining our two kinds of rich, exactly whom do Jesus and the other authors of Scripture have in mind when they offer such dire warnings? How is one to know if one's current level of wealth puts one in the crosshairs or not?

The Bible has an awful lot to say about money. I'm convinced that Scripture's focus on this topic has less to do with *riches* than *richness*. Perhaps we have confused the two, and the resultant attitudes have been a disaster for the church. Richness is often defined as a state of wealth. This simplistic description, however, seems to miss the points made by the illustrations of Matthew 25. Scripture puts much more focus on the attitudes and actions of those in a state of wealth.

> *Then He told them a parable: "A rich man's land was very productive. He thought to himself, 'What should I do, since I don't have anywhere to store my crops? I will do this,' he said. 'I'll tear down my barns and build bigger ones and store all my grain and my goods there. Then I'll say to myself, "You have many goods stored up for many years. Take it easy; eat, drink, and enjoy yourself."'*
>
> *"But God said to him, 'You fool! This very night your life is demanded of you. And the things you have prepared—whose will they be?'"*
>
> Luke 12:16–20

> *[Jesus] looked up and saw the rich dropping their offerings into the temple treasury. He also saw a poor widow dropping in two tiny coins. "I tell you the truth," He said. "This poor widow has put in more than*

all of them. For all these people have put in gifts out of their surplus, but she out of her poverty has put in all she had to live on."

Luke 21:1–4

Instruct those who are rich in the present age not to be arrogant or to set their hope on the uncertainty of wealth, but on God...

1 Timothy 6:17

Don't the rich oppress you and drag you into the courts?

James 2:6
(talking about the need to avoid
favouritism towards the rich)

Because you say, "I'm rich; I have become wealthy and need nothing," and you don't know that you are wretched, pitiful, poor, blind, and naked...

Revelation 3:17
(Jesus to the church in Laodicea)

The Pharisees, who were lovers of money, were listening to all these things and scoffing at Him.

Luke 16:14

This last verse is particularly instructive, for it links the characteristics of the Pharisees with those who love money.

What can we glean from these examples? I would suggest that "richness" is functionally described in Scripture as any of the following attributes in combination with one's wealth:

1. Self-sufficiency. The false confidence of being buffered or saved by one's stores of wealth (usually accompanied by self-pride and the assumption that I "earned it").
2. Entitlement. The expectation that the owning of wealth necessitates special treatment from others (see James 2:2–3).

3. Superiority. The belief that wealth actually makes one a better person.
4. Lack of generosity. Or apparent generosity that actually costs very little.

Are there any wealthy people in the Bible who don't come under condemnation? Well, yes... but not very many! Which probably speaks to the tremendous power of wealth, or its dogged pursuit (the love of money), to lead to richness. However, there are persons, such as Joseph of Arimethea, who donated the tomb for Christ, and Lydia of Thyatira, who hosted Paul and his fellow travellers in her house. The father figure in the parable of the prodigal son is a loving and forgiving man of great wealth. In the Old Testament, David and Job are two people who had great wealth and yet are remembered primarily for their intense devotion to God than their stockpile of possessions.

Now, here's the scary part. I may not count myself in "the five percent," and depending on my comparator I might even convince myself that I'm in the non-rich category. But do I ever have an attitude of self-sufficiency? Could I ever be described as entitled? Have I ever nurtured a sense of personal superiority? Do I ever fail to show true generosity? Yes. Yes. Yes. And yes. Repeatedly yes.

Simple self-reflection reveals the terrible truth: you don't have to be rich to have all the undesirable qualities of richness that are so abhorrent to God. So, are riches a hindrance to spiritual growth? Maybe not inherently so, but they sure can grease the wheels to richness, which is definitely a hindrance to God's work, in me and in our church.

What's the baggage that needs to be dropped? It might depend on whether you consider yourself in the rich or non-rich category. For the rich, it's time to stop feeling guilty for having been given five talents instead of two. That's the Master's plan, so don't be upset about it. Recognize, of course, that you'll certainly be accountable for the use of your talents and will have to fight every day against the tendency towards "richness."[10]

---

10 See Luggage Four for some practical thoughts on how to do this.

For the self-declared non-rich: will God hold the rich accountable for their stewardship? Indeed, He says that He will. In the meantime, God hasn't put any of us in the place to judge that accountability in the here and now. So no more judging people according to their car in the church parking lot. Let us never assume that riches automatically equal selfishness or lack of love in our wealthy brothers and sisters in Christ. And for those who got two talents instead of five, don't resent the rich. They have what they have because that's what the Master decided. In fact, for those in the two-talent situation, realize that we'll be held equally accountable for our investments of God's resources entrusted to our care. Let us be extra careful to examine ourselves and see if we're making the colossal mistake of having richness even without the riches!

Let's finish up this part by going back to one of the most famous sets of verses that speak to the link between wealth and un-spirituality. Almost everyone with any kind of church background will likely be familiar with these verses, but I bet very few can recite the stunning verse that follows along right after. Here's the familiar part, quoted in the opening of the present chapter:

> *Then Jesus said to His disciples, "I assure you: It will be hard for a rich person to enter the kingdom of heaven! Again I tell you, it is easier for a camel to go through the eye of a needle than for a rich person to enter the kingdom of God."*
>
> Matthew 19:23–24

Heard that before, right? But what happened next?

> *When the disciples heard this, they were utterly astonished and asked, "Then who can be saved?"*
>
> Matthew 19:25

In Jesus' time, I'm sure rich people were often honoured and considered worthy, so understandably the disciples were amazed at the idea that the rich would have a near impossible time getting into the Kingdom. But two thousand years later, in the church, we're all too familiar with those opening words of Jesus, which seem to confirm our now commonly held assumption of God's disdain for the rich.

But do you know the next verse, Matthew 19:26? It's part of this same exchange about riches and the Kingdom. I must admit, it wasn't until I seriously studied this passage that I even noticed how the dialogue ended. I once thought the camel comment was just a one-off warning from Jesus. I dare say the church has also truncated this passage when teaching about wealth, which is why we all know about the camel and the needle but not about what Jesus said next. Listen to Jesus' answer to the disciples' astonished question:

> But Jesus looked at them and said, "With men this is impossible, but with God all things are possible."
>
> Matthew 19:26

How did we ever manage to leave this ultra-important part of the conversation out of our collective memory?

Hear the whole teaching again through my paraphrase. Jesus said, "Yes, left unto him/herself, it will be nearly impossible for a rich man or woman to come to a place of complete personal surrender to God. Riches usually lead to richness. But with God, even this can be overcome, such that riches can be used without richness, by the ones to whom He gives them, for His ordained purposes and ultimate glory."

If you ask me, that statement is worth reading twice.

Even if you think you're in "the ninety-nine percent."

Heavenly Father,

Every generous act and perfect gift is from You, Father of lights. Because I know You, I am richly blessed even if not rich.

Forgive me for my attitude of self-reliance, my comfort in my abilities, and all selfish pride that may accompany my apparent achievements.

Forgive me for my attitude of entitlement, for the ungrounded assumption that I deserve better than what I have.

Forgive me for my frequent sense of personal superiority and for the oppression of others, which results when I exalt myself at another's expense.

Forgive me for my pervasive lack of generosity and unwillingness to share the very things You are sharing with me.

Forgive my judgmental spirit, which seeks to hold others to their accounts all the while usurping Your position as the Master who assigned the accounts in the first place.

Open my eyes to the Kingdom investment opportunities You have set before me, the means of multiplying your gifts that I might return to You all, or even more than, You have entrusted to me.

Replace my selfish heart with Your generous nature, which freely causes rain to fall on the righteous and the unrighteous.

Protect me from the temptations to go from rich to richness.

Help me to have the courage to act in such a way that I might one day hear, "Well done, good and faithful slave! You were faithful over a few things; I will put you in charge of many things. Share your master's joy!" Amen.

Luggage Three

"I need to figure out God's specific will for my life."

If there is any chapter I am most afraid of writing, it's this one. Since the time of the early church, armies of theologians have scoured Scripture, retranslated, debated, postulated, theorized, and formulated paradigms that seek to capture the essence of "God's will" and how it relates to us. I've done a lot of reading around the topic and have found that some of the arguments become so nuanced and convoluted that even a university-educated, serious-minded person can easily become fatigued and cynical as to whether a single, coherent paradigm even exists.

Bring up "God's will" in a church setting and the Pandora's box metaphor quickly becomes relevant. Terms like predestination, unconditional election, Molinism, universalism, fatalism, Calvinism, restrictive inclusivism, and so on all come into play. I really don't know the right answer, and there's no way I could write a summary of the field, nor am I qualified to do so. Yet this is something every serious Christian thinks about at one time or another. It's not sufficient to just throw up one's hands in frustration and give up because we feel confused by the theologians' differing interpretations. Therefore, as in previous chapters, I'm deliberately staying away from controversy and interpretation. I'm not even going to talk about seeking God's will—the fact that we should do so is already pretty straightforward. I will focus instead on the practical attitudes many of us in the church have adopted when it comes to matters of God's will.

Almost since the beginning of the Christian church, God's will has been sought with varying degrees of sincerity and then used or abused to perpetrate all kinds of interesting and sometimes despicable actions. This practice certainly shows no sign of disappearing today. Even our kids figure out at a young age that you can get away with a lot of stuff if you appeal to an apparently absent higher authority.

> "Why are you eating that chocolate bar right before supper?"
> "Um… Mom said I could."
> "But Mom's been out all day. When did she say that?"
> "I don't remember… but she did say I could have it any time I want it."

Right.

Anyone who's spent time in a church family has undoubtedly heard stories of God's will ranging from the mundane ("I really felt God wanted me to score that goal to win the game") to the inspirational ("I came to believe God wanted me to give my life to this people group") to the truly bizarre (way too many examples to mention). When you hear about someone who has recently "found" God's will, if you're like me, your response ranges from admiration (if someone surrenders to doing a thankless job) to skepticism (if someone decides to march around a brothel until it spontaneously falls down) to outright disgust ("God told me it's His will to leave my wife for this other woman").

Perhaps it's part of my own baggage that I immediately get my back up when someone starts a sentence by saying, "I think it's God's will that I…" No matter how that sentence ends, my internal response is almost always, "Hmmmmmmmmm." I actually feel sorry for God, if that's possible. So many things are done in His name and reported as being His will. I can only wonder what fraction of them actually reflect His character and desire for His creation.

As serious Christ-followers, let's put aside the war stories about crazy or seemingly irrational things some people understand as being God's will. For sure, let's dispense with the overtly sinful and unscriptural actions some claim as God's will, usually as a means to justify their own will. Let's focus on the issue of His will as it pertains to the daily lives of us regular people.

To start, here's a smattering of verses that seem to imply God has a specific will for each one of us:

A man's steps are established by the Lord, and He takes pleasure in his way.

Psalm 37:23

"For I know the plans I have for you"—this is the Lord's declaration—"plans for your welfare, not for disaster, to give you a future and a hope."

Jeremiah 29:11

Since man's days are determined and the number of his months depends on You...

Job 14:5

I certainly do not dispute the words of Scripture! But most authors and teachers I've heard will use these verses to launch into a discussion about determining exactly what His will is going to be for each of us. A brief internet search reveals a multitude of online resources dedicated to helping you "find God's will for your life." I'm not mocking this; many of the articles are written by wise teachers, and their advice on the process of seeking seems absolutely biblical and spot-on.

However, the underlying assumption common to all this advice is that there's one specific "will" out there—as specific as tickets to a vacation destination. For example, if I book a flight to Charleston, South Carolina, I expect the plane to end up in Charleston, South Carolina. If the plane flies to Charleston, West Virginia, that's not the same thing and I won't be happy; it will cost me time and money to redirect and arrive at the intended destination. If the plane flies to Sydney, Australia, that would be considered a massive navigational failure that would ruin my entire vacation—although I do love Sydney, so maybe that's not the best example.

Here's the question: do we as Christians assume from the verses above and expect, based on other people's stories, that God has a single "destination" for us in all circumstances if we're truly "in His will"? And do we assume that if we somehow arrive at the wrong destination, all is lost?

Whoa. Now I've gone too far, right? Please read my proposition again, carefully. Are we sure God has just one multi-step pathway set out for us in every single situation? Is it really like my kids' Mario Brothers video game, where I can only move left to right, hopping across pillars to get to the castle and avoid falling in the moat?

Again, without question, there are many examples in the Bible of situations where God clearly had a singular purpose for a specific person. Noah, Joshua, Gideon, Moses, Jonah, David... seriously, the first two-thirds of the Old Testament reads like a chronicle of God telling specific people to do specific things in a specific way. Both Mary and Joseph are examples of New Testament people who received detailed, direct tasks from

God (such as their instructions to flee to Egypt with the infant Jesus). We don't fully understand the exact way in which God communicated His instructions to many of these individuals. Therefore, one can't be faulted for at least considering the possibility that God really does have specific intentions for us at times.

On the other hand, the writings of the New Testament present a slightly different view of individual people. The people of the New Testament aren't just God's emissaries, prophets, kings, and warriors; I'm not saying the Old Testament is exclusively so, but one can't ignore the fact that in the setting of the Gospels, Jesus was surrounded by and interacted with countless unnamed people—the man with a demon, the rich young ruler, the Roman centurion, the man blind from birth, etc. Paul also mentions many early Christ-followers, some by name, others by trade. For most, we know little to nothing about their lives and character apart from a single verse or two about something they did.

What kind of direction did these nameless people get from Jesus? Seriously, who wouldn't like a chance to stand in front of Jesus in person and have Him tell you exactly what He wants you to do?

Let's have a look at the outcome for a couple people who did have that opportunity.

The Rich Young Ruler (see Matthew 19:16–21)

The ruler asked, "Teacher, what good must I do to have eternal life?" In other words, what's Your will for my life?
"Keep the commandments," Jesus said.
"Which ones?"
Jesus then listed some of the Ten Commandments.
"Done," the ruler said. "What else must I do?"
"Sell your belongings, give to the poor, and follow Me."

We all know that the rich young man left, because he didn't want to do what Jesus suggested. Still, look at what Jesus said. Was it any different than what He had said to others? Not really. Anyone who listened to the sermon on the mount could have taken those same instructions. I bet the rich young man was probably hoping Jesus would give him some kind of single, specific, heroic task, like "Raise money to build a beautiful extension to the temple" or "Go start a home for lepers." I bet the young man would have loved it, too: a good, specific challenge with promise of reward. But what was Jesus' apparent will for his life? "Follow Me and let the actions of your life show it."

The Woman Caught in Adultery (see John 8:1–11)

I recognize that some scholars debate whether this account was added to John's gospel at a later date, but Jesus' words are very much in keeping with the other accounts of His interactions with people. When the woman was brought to Jesus, He didn't condemn her; He sent her accusers away and then told her His will: "Go and sin no more." He didn't ask her to start a ministry for prostitutes or abused women, although if she did so it would have fit nicely with His character and reflected His concern for the oppressed. No, His only specific advice was to leave behind her old way of living. What happens after that, well, one can only imagine her life would have been forever changed if she really did start afresh.

The Roman Centurion (see Matthew 8:5–13)

This is one of my favourite stories. A Roman centurion recognizes that Jesus is no ordinary man, that He commands fantastic powers over non-human entities, and that He is good. Jesus calls out the religious people around him by saying that this agent of the occupying government actually has greater faith than any of the chosen of Israel. How's that for a commendation! He then tells the centurion, "Go, your servant is healed."

I'd love to know what happened in the centurion's life after that. Do you think he was changed by his encounter with Jesus? Do you think he followed the story of Jesus' doings in the community? Do you think he told other men in the army about what happened? I wonder if he joined the early church a couple of years later? I suppose Jesus could have called him to leave the army (although He would have known that would be certain death for the centurion, as a deserter). Jesus could have told him to at least try to protect the local Israelites. But no, none of that. Jesus' apparent will for that centurion, who was praised for his faith, was to just go back to what he was doing… as a changed man, no doubt.

The Demon-Possessed Man (see Luke 8:26–39)

After being healed by Jesus,

The man from whom the demons had departed kept begging Him to be with Him. But He sent him away and said, "Go back to your home, and tell all that God has done for you." And off he went, proclaiming throughout the town all that Jesus had done for him.

Luke 8:38–39

Wow. Here's a guy, healed by Jesus, who desperately wants to hear, "Follow Me." It sounds like this guy was ready to do anything; he was begging for Jesus to keep him, use him. But what was Jesus' will for him? "Go on back home and carry on, but glorify God in your interactions with your community." So the man did it. Without asking if Jesus specifically wanted him to organize an evangelistic speaker series or distribute pamphlets. How exactly did the healed man do what Jesus asked? We don't really know, other than that he didn't seem to need further instructions.

Sending Out the Seventy-Two (Luke 10:1–9)

I don't know if I've ever heard a sermon on this passage; it seems to be somewhat ignored, perhaps because there isn't an immediately obvious life lesson. Basically Jesus chooses seventy-two people and sends them out ahead of Him to announce the arrival of the Kingdom of God. He gives a few general instructions about traveling (don't get distracted, try to stay in one place, and eat whatever they put in front of you; that would be a really tough one for me), but otherwise he just wants them to heal the sick and tell them God has come into the very midst of Israel. Now, off you go! No mention of exactly which town to go to, which house to stay at, how long to stay, who should accompany whom, etc.

◆　◆　◆

Sometimes I think Jesus was downright unconcerned with petty details. If I can paraphrase Luke 12:13–14, a man calls out to Jesus, "Teacher, my brother and I are arguing about our inheritance. Tell my brother to be fair and give me my share!" How does Jesus reply? I love it: first, He calls him a "friend," then basically says, "It's not really My place to be an arbitrator here. Go figure it out yourself, but be careful not to be greedy." Reminds me of some of my own parenting moments, such as when I'm tired of having to judge and negotiate arguments between my kids. "Go sort it out yourselves! You're going to have to learn how to get along with people at some point!" Jesus was much more concerned about the *way* in which that guy went about his life than the actual details. He refused to give any kind of direction as to the settling of the matter of the estate.

Did you ever wonder how the apostles figured out what to *do* as the early church got started? How did Paul know he should take all those exact missionary journeys? Nowhere does he actually say that God "told him" where and when to go on each trip, or exactly how long to stay. I'm sure he prayed about it, and probably listened to the counsel and requests of other Christians. At some point, Paul simply had to make a decision and go with it, trusting that God was going to use him wherever he went. Which is exactly what happened in the end.

My first personal encounter with this principle came through one of my university friends, Rob. One summer, Rob received requests to work at two different Christian summer camps. Obviously, he couldn't do both and had to make a decision. I remember him telling me how he agonized over the options, praying frequently and weighing both positions in many ways. You might not think this was an earth-shaking decision, but Rob honestly wanted to make sure he was doing what God wanted. Eventually, after a few weeks, Rob came to me and said that he just didn't feel as though he had an answer from God. I didn't have any insight, so I left him to further contemplation.

A few days later, Rob came back with a smile on his face, telling me that he'd finally found peace with the decision.

"Did you hear from God?" I asked.

"No," Rob replied, "but I realized that both options will give me the chance to serve God with my summer, and that's really what He asks of me. So I just chose the one that seemed to make the most sense."

That summer, we worked together at the same camp and I got to see Rob make a huge impact in the lives of a few young men—an impact that carried on long past the end of summer.

As you can see, I've never forgotten that lesson. Maybe God's biggest concern is that our decisions fall in line with who He wants us to be rather than just precisely what we think He wants us to do or where He wants us to go.

So where does the baggage issue come in on this one? Sometimes I think we can become fearful that we're not hearing God's voice or seeing His direction for a specific decision. We can get so fixated on the idea that there's one, semi-concealed pathway God expects us to find. We get frustrated when we don't feel as though we've found that path. Then we get fearful that choosing the wrong path will result in some calamity because we didn't find God's will. The final result is often paralysis. We don't know what to do, so we do nothing.

Here is the accompanying attitudinal baggage we might not consciously consider but which is very much the logical outworking of fear and paralysis on the issue of God's will: we somehow forget that God loves to restore, reconcile, recreate, and renew. It certainly is possible that a poor decision can be made without adequate thought, prayer, and counsel, but that doesn't mean God can't shape the outcome to ultimately fall within His will again, especially if His will is primarily defined as His will for who we are.

In other words, God's will for our present and future isn't thwarted by our bad decisions. Just because you made a mistake in the past, big or small, doesn't mean you're permanently deviated from His will. Rather, His will for your life moving forward starts with what you've got and where you are now. And it's still focussed on becoming like Jesus.

I've learned this in a very personal way. When I was a resident in internal medicine, the time came when I had to choose a subspecialty. Throughout residency, I'd loved endocrinology and without question that was what I wanted to do. But I didn't really pray about it. I didn't wonder if that was the best use of God's opportunities for me in medicine. I didn't even seek counsel from anybody. It was just what I wanted to do, so I did it.

For years afterward, I struggled with guilt, wondering if I had veered off God's plan for my life. Don't get me wrong, I still loved my career, but I wondered if maybe I should have been an infectious disease specialist or intensivist or generalist or gastroenterologist. Their skills seemed so much more useful in developing nations. I wondered if I had made a mistake and now God's plan was ruined because I would never be any use on a mission field.

How utterly wrong I was. In 2013, God opened my eyes. I received a call out of the blue asking if I would come teach endocrinology to a group of nationally trained Cameroonian physicians who were in a unique, Christian-based internal medicine program at Mbingo Baptist Hospital. It was a wonderful two weeks. The student physicians were fantastic learners who graciously accepted my teaching and mentoring. Much to my surprise, it seemed like the floodgates of African endocrinology opened while I was there! Patients with diabetes, thyroid diseases, infertility, adrenal diseases, pituitary disorders, metabolic bone disease—the full breadth of my specialty, children and adults alike—started appearing as if out of nowhere. At times, I was literally running from one ward to another, then over to the clinic and back to the ward because people were calling for endocrinology consultations. I was humbled to hear that word had gotten out; people were driving eight hours to see someone who was likely the only endocrinologist in the country. And here I thought African medicine was just malaria, HIV, and trauma surgery.

God used me in those two weeks—on the very bridge I thought I had burned.

If I could go back to my residency, I hope I would approach my decision differently—with prayer, discussion, and consideration of my wider career picture. In retrospect, though, was it God's will for me to do endocrinology subspecialty training? I'm not sure that question even matters, to tell the truth. The point is, I want to follow God's will now, in who I am and what I do, and God has proven that He can take whatever I've got and make it fit perfectly within His wider will for my present and future.

There's one more aspect to this baggage about finding God's will we need to consider.

I suspect we sometimes muddy the waters by seeking God's will for a situation where it's already right in front of our nose. Every now and then, I've heard someone wonder aloud about God's will for a certain action, then express complete ambivalence or mystification about what it might be. I have certainly done this myself. As just one example, someone with medical training once said to me, "I've been asked to volunteer to go to Africa for a few weeks and help out at a Christian mission station. I'm just not sure if it's really His will." Guess what? If you're presented with a specific need for which you are uniquely suited and volunteering on that mission station is done with a cheerful heart and for the support of God's work, then of course it's God's will for you to go, unless there is some other equally Kingdom-oriented reason not to. Helping to meet the needs of people God brings in our path is hardly ever *against* God's will.

I suspect this way of thinking will be new and uncomfortable for many of us, since we're so used to the idea that God's will is something mystical and hidden, only ever revealed by months of fasting, prayer, and waiting for specific scriptural passages that miraculously come to our attention.

As always, insincere people will be able to twist "God's will" to suit their own will. But for the serious Christ-follower, there's really no getting around the fact that if God puts in front of you an opportunity to partner in His work, and especially if it falls within your particular resources and gifts, it's going to be hard to argue that it isn't His will to take it up. That doesn't mean we don't talk to God about it or ask the counsel of wise fellow Christ-followers if there really is a question. I'm also not saying we won't find ourselves in situations when it's difficult to immediately know what God would have us do; those will require much prayer and seeking. But let's stop thinking that we need to hold off on the simple actions of living out our faith until we see if it's His will. I suspect this should be the rule rather than the exception.

Some final thoughts. Why did Jesus give the sermon on the mount, anyway? Was He just outlining the new laws that would eventually become enshrined in various monastic orders and rules, which in turn have been passed down to us in some very legalistic forms? As Dallas Willard so nicely explains in his book, *The Divine Conspiracy,* Jesus wasn't just laying out new regulations for life but rather explaining and describing to the people what the Kingdom of God looked like... which is really to say, what God's will looks like.[11]

If I want to know God's will, I need look no further than the character and Kingdom of God, because His will will always be a reflection of His character, displayed in us. And if I want to know what God wants me to do, I need only consider the actions that naturally flow from imitating Him in everything I do with the people around me. Will He direct specific actions at specific times? Quite possibly, and careful thought, prayer, and godly counsel will be helpful in discerning those times. But the focus, the big picture of His will—day to day, month to month, and year to year—neither changes nor needs special insight or miraculous signs. Just know Him, love Him, strive to become like Him, act like Him. In everything. And the actions come last, as they are a natural outflowing of becoming like Him.

Heavenly Father,

You have shown me what is good and what You require of me: to live justly, love mercy, and walk humbly by Your side. How often I fail at those three things, preferring instead to focus on the details of the task at hand.

Without question, I want to follow Your leading in every step of my life. I want to do Your will.

Help me to focus firstly on imitating You. Give me wisdom in my decisions such that my actions become a natural and automatic expression of Your desire for my life and community.

Relieve me of any fears or inactions that result from waiting upon more instructions than You have decided I need.

For the decisions I have made thus far, please renew, recreate, restore, redirect, and rebuild, so that I may go on my way, proclaiming You throughout the town. Amen.

11 Dallas Willard, *The Divine Conspiracy: Rediscovering Our Hidden Life in God* (San Francisco, CA: Harper, 1998).

Luggage Four

"I need to try harder to be
a good Christian."

A couple of years ago, a few of my buddies persuaded me to join them for a three-day intensive golf school in Phoenix. I've messed around with golf since I was a teenager but have never had any formal lessons and it shows. For me, golf is all about goofing around with the guys for a couple hours, but I did agree that it would be nice to be a more skilled player. So off I went with the high hope of breaking eighty. Or a hundred.

On day one, we started off by meeting our super relaxed (and maybe slightly bored) golf instructor. While waiting for us, we saw him hit a few balls with the driver; each one about two hundred yards, down the middle of the fairway. Which was fairly impressive, considering he was taking sips from a coffee held in one hand. Anyhow, after introductions, he asked us all a question: "What makes you guys want to spend money trying to play the most difficult and frustrating sport in the world?" Great question. I didn't have an answer then, and I don't have one now. And yet, I golf.

I worked really hard those three days—in the classroom, driving range, putting green, sand traps, and deep rough. I undertook endless exercises, practice swings, and self-analysis. The final result: after intensive training, I became really good at being able to tell other people what they were doing wrong. My own golf game? Marginal improvement. Now I'm back to goofing around with trick balls and a laser pointer on my putter head.

But I tried really, really hard. I did. I took it seriously, listened carefully, and focussed intently before every swing. The good golfers out there will be smirking now, saying that three days of intensive schooling won't change anything, that I need to be practicing and playing every day. I'm sure there's some truth to that, but I remain convinced that even if I gave up everything and golfed every day for the next five years, I probably couldn't win even a local club tournament. No matter how hard I try, it seems impossible to get the major improvements I would really like to see.

Ever feel that way after reading the Bible? Or hearing a sermon? I've heard an awful lot of great speakers preach brilliant sermons about some aspect of Christian living. The "take home" usually comes along the lines of "Now get out there and put it into action!" Yeah! Except I can't, or at least not with any real consistency.

I think this situation is also prevalent among novice Bible readers, like myself. So many parts of the Bible seem at first to be instructions to "do this" and "don't do that." These kinds of lists almost seem to be begging to be made into a code of conduct.

When I was a university student, one of my friends talked me into attending a weekend retreat hosted by a conservative preacher. In the space of sixteen hours, he took almost every scripture I'd ever heard and turned it into a "principle" (read: rule) for Christian living. Thinking back, I can't remember some of the scriptural backings, but I remember the rules! "Don't listen to music with drums in it," "A girl must never be alone with a boy until there's a wedding ring on her finger," etc. We even got a hardcover book with pictures in case we were too dumb to understand the words. Sadly for him, I recently read that this brother has had to step down from his ministry due to what ultimately turned out to be an inability to follow these very same rules.

This issue really hit home during a Bible study discussion with my small group. We were studying Philippians and listening to a speaker whom I really respect. That night's session included the following verse: *"in humility consider others as more important than yourselves"* (Philippians 2:3). The speaker did a good job of illustrating how important this is, how this mentality is totally absent in our culture, and how radical it would be if people actually lived that way. We discussed it as a group, and of course everyone agreed the speaker had made excellent points.

Then I asked a question: "How exactly do we do it?"

Complete silence. For several minutes. I repeated the question, but still silence. Why? I think it was because we all realized there was no chip we could insert into our brains' frontal lobes to upgrade our character to one of considering others more important than ourselves. Think about it. There are truly no answers. Examples, yes, but life is too complex to be explained and planned based on a few examples. At best, someone might squeak out, "Try harder…" We all know how that ends: with a quadruple bogey on the par three.

That discussion started a chain of events for me, thinking about the whole issue of "trying harder" in the Christian life.

Some of you might be thinking this chapter is really about overcoming legalism. We could have a good discussion about the role of God's law in showing us our sins (Romans 3:19–20), but this goes way beyond the theology of law versus grace. It goes beyond considering the means by which we are to avoid the don'ts. I'm talking about the admonishments and descriptions of how we are to do the dos.

Remember these verses?

Do everything without grumbling or arguing.

Philippians 2:14

Pray constantly. Give thanks for everything…

1 Thessalonians 5:17–18

Do not judge…

Matthew 7:1

… don't worry about tomorrow…

Matthew 6:34

… love your enemies and pray for those who persecute you…

Matthew 5:44

Here's a confession. After thirty-eight years of hearing this taught to me, I can't claim to have accomplished any of these directives. At least, not consistently, and in fact it's downright rare that I could examine my heart and say, "Yeah, I don't grumble anymore!" No matter how hard I (intermittently) try. It's now to the point where my eyes glaze over and I start to tune out when I hear a speaker give a pep talk on some biblically recommended character trait I already know I can't just "switch on."

The idea that we need to work on changing ourselves to conform to the scriptural model is one tough piece of baggage to drop. I'd go so far as to say that in North America, our culture is totally addicted to self-help, pep talks, and the notion that hard work with sheer determination is all it takes to make anything happen. The church is certainly not immune to this manner of thinking. Unlike stories of successful weight loss, when was the last time your pastor invited someone up front to tell the congregation how they have successfully and completely abolished all worry, forever?

Probably never, because I doubt anyone would have the chutzpah to make such a bold and ludicrous claim.

Here's the interesting part. Jesus knew this would be the case and warned His disciples, "By the way, you're not going to be able to do what I just said." That's my paraphrase of John 15:5, admittedly lifted out of its fuller context. But He did say it: *"You can do nothing without Me."* I think we need to hear that section of the verse on a daily basis, because we're so quick to focus on our own efforts at doing everything.

Of course, this verse wasn't some backhanded putdown. To better understand why He said this, we need to look at the whole account surrounding that verse. This brings us to one of the most familiar passages in all Scripture. In fact, it's so familiar that I'm reluctant to write about it for fear of simply adding more noise to the cacophony of commentaries already out there.

This is the passage in which Jesus says, "Abide in Me." Most translations of John 15:1–10 use the words "abide" or "remain in." I don't speak Greek, so I can't comment on the suitability of the translation. Since most English translations use those words, I guess nobody has any better ideas!

The problem is that the sentence doesn't make inherent, immediate sense to me. If someone I met said, "Hey, you need to abide in me," I would have no clue what they meant. What did Jesus mean? He did elaborate by metaphorically describing Himself as "the vine" and us as "the branches," but still, what does that exactly signify for day-to-day living? Here are a couple of other commentators' thoughts of what it means to abide in Him:

1. Become a Christian (specifically, believe in Jesus).
2. Depend on Jesus/trust God.
3. Persevere in the faith.
4. Obey Jesus' commands.
5. Rest in Him (or rather, have a relationship with Him).

All of these sound good, and aren't necessarily mutually exclusive. In some sense, I'm sure these are essentially getting at the right idea. Remember, I'm not a Bible scholar and don't claim any superior insight, but the little knot I get in my stomach when I read these interpretations arises from the fact that I'm again seeing a list of things I need to work on, to do better. And when I try harder, *in my own strength*, to obey Jesus' commands, it doesn't often work out.

If I may offer a humble opinion, there are only three things I've found that I *can* offer God when faced with His truth: praise, confession, or submission. In the topic at hand, submission would be the most appropriate. Just like Jesus said, *"You can do nothing without Me."* Submission of my will, my desires, my time, my resources, my personality. The fruit (the changes in me) can only be brought about by the work of the Holy Spirit after handing over the controls (abiding in Him). The fruit is borne on the branches only because they receive their life and nutrients through being a mere extension of the vine.

Just to be clear, this biblical principle of change wrought by the Spirit after surrendering our lives to Him is not an insight I claim to have realized on my own. You can read this in the writings of many excellent Christian authors. Dallas Willard does a masterful job of showing that the rules and behaviours apparently demanded by Jesus in His sermon on the mount are best understood as examples of what He'll make us like in His Kingdom, as He changes us, rather than a set of unattainable character changes we are expected to spontaneously cause in ourselves and by ourselves.

Somehow, along the way, I have missed this teaching, believing instead that it was just up to me to try harder.

You know what makes it worse? All the so-called nonbelievers who seem to show more of those highly desirable Christ-like qualities than I do! This seems to increase the weight of the impossible self-improvement baggage.

For many years, I had a colleague who was quite open about the fact that she was a humanist and felt that the claims of the Bible were simply ridiculous (although she had a very polite way of saying so). Apart from that, she was easily the nicest, most caring, conscientious, non-confrontational lover of people I have ever met. And everyone knew it. She was almost famous for her incredible kindness. Whenever faced with a nasty, abusive, or angry patient, it was common to hear other doctors advise, "Send them to see Jill. She'll be able to handle them." And it was true. Jill picked up a couple of patients who were literally driving me crazy, even scaring me with their threatening behaviour. In her hands, these hard patients seemed to turn into little lost puppies, glad to have found their way home.

Good for her. Maddening for me. Why couldn't I be like that? Why can't I just smile and nod sympathetically when someone unfairly blames me for something that's made them unhappy? Why is it so often a struggle to remain patient and cheerful when someone makes unreasonable demands of my time? Why can I not keep my mouth shut when faced with the opportunity to contribute to a discussion that's strictly about complaining?

Why not? Pretty simple, actually: because I can be hurt, I can be annoyed, and I like to complain and shift blame onto others. Afterwards, I usually kick myself for being so easily led into an attitude or action I profess to be trying to avoid. But there it is. I haven't been able to change myself purely through my own efforts.

Now, to be clear, I'm not saying that we just pray a simple, one-time prayer of submission and then never bother to worry about our character and actions again. There is value to the practice of memorizing and meditating upon verses like Luke 12:22–32 (Jesus' admonition not to worry). There is value in setting goals and asking others to help us be accountable to our actions. Remember, trying really hard to be a good golf player doesn't necessarily guarantee any improvement or success, but failure to swing the club at all ensures you never leave the first tee.

Some of the other baggage mentioned in the book thus far is more easily dropped. This one is really tough, probably because I'll never achieve perfection in my lifetime. But let's remember exactly what baggage we're talking about. The baggage is not my character flaws; that's just inherent. The baggage is the thought that I have to make myself change, and the expectation that I can read something in the Bible and "just do it" all the time, if I try harder.

"You can do nothing without Me," Jesus said.

I want to stop complaining. Action: surrender my complaining heart to God, to be changed by Him. I want to stop gossiping. Action: surrender my gossipy mind to God, to be changed by Him. I want to consider others more important than myself. Action: surrender my pride to God, to be changed by Him. I want to love my neighbour. Action: surrender my selfish heart to God, to be changed by Him. I want to drop this baggage of expecting change by trying harder in my own strength. Action: surrender my whole life and character to God, to be changed by Him.

He never promised we would be instantly perfected the moment we gave our lives to Him; it's a continual process of prayerful surrender and resurrender. Confession and repentance when we fail, then asking Him to change us as we get ready to swing the club again. That's abiding in Him. His process of changing our hearts will be far more effective and durable than our brief attempts to do it on our own.

Heavenly Father,

I want to be perfect, as You are perfect. Yet I'm so far away from that and often moving in the wrong direction. I do not understand what I'm doing, because I don't practice what I want to do. Instead I do what I hate. Somehow I'm amazed to discover my own powerlessness to change my heart.

Please release me from the pride of thinking that I can do the things You want to do in me. Please free me from the incredibly unnecessary guilt that weighs me down as I come to terms with the parts of me that behave as though I'm still enslaved to sin.

As I surrender my character and heart to Your changes, set me free from the actions and thoughts of my old nature.

I present my life to You for re-creation, in Your image and by Your hands.

Thank you, Jesus, that this is even possible for a recalcitrant and resistant heart like mine, a heart I so often choose to keep for myself. Until now. Amen.

Luggage Five

"It's important to be a Christian
so you can go to heaven."

"It's important to be a Christian so you can go to heaven." What? How can a true statement like that be classified as baggage?

As a child, I remember thinking about this idea of heaven. My childhood church wasn't even a fire-and-brimstone type, so I can't say I was ever threatened with hell, yet from my earliest remembrance I distinctly recall knowing that if you want to go to heaven after you die, you need to become a Christian now.

Just as an aside, I really dislike the phrase "become a Christian." It might have held significant meaning back in AD 100, but it's devoid of clarity today. It might mean nothing more than "attend church" or even just "culturally identify with the traditional Judeo- Christian ethic." Being called a "believer" is definitely too ambiguous. A believer of what? Sometimes it's a code word between Christians who are discussing state secrets in the marketplace, like who to get to unplug your drain—"If you need your sink fixed, you should really call this plumber… he's a believer." Wink-wink. If you really want a good code phrase, though, I suggest "He's a brother" or "She's a sister." That keeps it really subtle, and focussed on the secret club aspects of church membership. Please note the sarcasm.

I think "follower of Jesus" is probably the most workable current phrase, although that sounds passive, too, and is open to different understanding. Actually, "a slave of Jesus Christ" might be the best term I can think of, but probably won't attract positive responses from those who are seriously investigating Christianity, let alone from society as a whole. So for the purpose of this chapter, I'm going to use the familiar term "become a Christian" as synonymous with "become a slave of Jesus."

I wonder how many Christians out there became Christians solely out of fear of a tormented afterlife. That may well be true for some, but it's probably fair to say this motivation might have played a bigger part in centuries past, when official excommunication from the church was considered a threat grave enough to set countries to war.

I once visited the Basilica di Santa Maria del Fiore, a magnificent cathedral in Florence, Italy. It's one of my favourite buildings because it was built by Brunelleschi, a self-taught architect, artist, and all-around smart guy who just figured out how to erect the massive masonry dome all by himself, a feat still considered almost superhuman more than five hundred years later. It's truly beautiful to behold from a distance, but the interior of the dome is one of the most terrifying and disturbing ceiling frescoes you could imagine. It's basically a huge collection of scenes depicting the last judgement and the awful tortures and degradations of hell—or what passed for hell in the minds of the artists (definitely lacking in biblical support). It's really difficult to even look at, despite being considered a Renaissance masterpiece.

To his credit, it wasn't Brunelleschi's idea to have a Renaissance horror movie playing on the ceiling of his magnificent dome. One wonders why the city fathers/building patrons/church leaders, who were all the same people, chose that subject as the cathedral's centrepiece. It becomes obvious when you think about it: the threat of hell was the trump card for keeping people in line with God's rules—more likely, the church rules. "Welcome to church, we're glad you're here. Listen to what the priest says, and in case you're thinking of ignoring what he tells you, just have a quick glance at the ceiling…" Problem solved.

Today, of course, we're much more modernized. Belief in the afterlife is considered mystical thinking at best, and mention of some kind of post-life torment is thought of as downright bad-mannered, a sure sign of being a brainwashed simpleton. A few years back, one of our local politicians in Alberta made the bad decision to use the phrase "lake of fire" to support one of his opinions against an issue related to same-sex unions, much to the delight of the press.

I don't intend to get into a discussion of the potential physical versus spiritual characteristics of hell. There are some very interesting and differing opinions you can read, if curious. However, even a sanitized definition of hell as "non-heaven" is an unattractive concept to Christians. Some kinds of hell doctrine are present in most denominational belief statements.

Fear of hell may not be a common reason for new believers to come to Christ anymore, but it's still a common motivation for current believers to engage in evangelism. And rightly so! This brings me back to the original question, as to whether becoming a Christian for the purpose of attainment of heaven can even be considered baggage.

But here is the central point of the chapter. Has assurance of salvation, popularly defined as a reservation to heaven, left us with the baggage of spiritual complacency? "It's important to be a Christian so I can go to heaven. And since I am a Christian, now I'm set. I don't have to be concerned with much else."

Just as there's no biblical support for the depictions of hell made by Renaissance artists, so is there no biblical support for the notion that becoming a Christian is a one-off decision to sign an afterlife insurance policy. Rather, becoming a Christian, as defined by Jesus Himself, means living an abundant life with Christ *now*, throughout our time on earth, with heaven as the natural extension of our eternal future. I'll happily await that glorious life in heaven, but my deliberate ignorance of the discipleship and abundant life now part is the baggage that concerns me.

Jesus didn't make discipleship an option for our consideration. *"If anyone wants to come with Me, he must deny himself, take up his cross, and follow Me"* (Matthew 16:24). The words "must" (not "is highly recommended") and "take up his cross" imply some degree of difficult work or sacrifice on our part. So what exactly is discipleship, this work Jesus asks of us?

A detailed examination of discipleship is well beyond the scope of this book, but my understanding of it could be best expressed as "a process of complete engagement of one's heart, mind, time, and resources with Jesus and His Kingdom." There may be other definitions out there that emphasize different aspects; regardless, I want to make a point about what discipleship largely isn't: showing up at church every Sunday morning.

My pastor friends might have a few palpitations from my suggestion that Sunday attendance isn't synonymous with the process outlined above. Before I get booted off the elders board, let me clarify that there are many good reasons to attend church regularly (see Luggage Nine), yet simply showing up doesn't equal the complete life-engagement Jesus asks of us.

Again, a complete discussion of how to be discipled is better described by other authors than I. Next time you're volunteering in the church nursery and need to duck out for that extra-long bathroom break, head over to the library; you'll probably find a shelf full of discipleship how-to books. My focus is only on our attitude towards the work required of us to participate in the process of discipleship.

But wait, didn't the last chapter focus on our inability to make ourselves become changed through our own power? Yes. Notice the difference:

discipleship isn't about us changing ourselves, it's about putting in the effort to engage our whole self with Jesus, so that He can produce the fruit.

And it's going to be inconvenient. Carrying crosses is rarely mistaken for a vacation. That's why disciple and discipline are kind of the same thing. Discipleship is more than just studying the Bible or learning the faith. It's the complete engagement of our lives with Jesus and what He's doing.

Think about the mission trip that gets organized but only three people sign up. Think about the Wednesday night Old Testament Bible study that gets offered but only one person registers. Think about the Sunday morning announcement requesting more youth sponsors which only one volunteer responds to—the lady who's already running the children's ministry. Hey, before you start feeling judged by what I'm saying, don't worry... I've been a non-responder, non-participant myself. We're all in this together.

I'm certainly not saying that the true disciple is the one who volunteers for every single ministry and service the church offers. But I do ask myself why people don't show more willingness to engage with building their relationship with God and being part of Kingdom work. After much reflection, soul-searching, and probing of the mind, I think I know the answer: we don't want to.

Let me press a little harder. How much time do I spend really reading and digesting God's Word? Well, it depends who's playing in the hockey game. How much time do I spend talking to God—not just listing requests, but actually pouring out my heart and then listening? Well, it depends upon how sick I'm feeling and how worried I am about what's going to happen. How often do I call up that person who I know is struggling and really needs someone to talk to? Well, it depends on if I'm feeling busy from work or not. Why don't I make a more conscious effort to do these things?

Because I don't want to.

Why don't I want to?

Because I mostly want to do the things I want to do.

It sounds so juvenile, but for myself, I know it's as simple as that. Now, before we become awash in guilt or legalism, let's just pause to reflect on some of the things that comprise the disciplines of Christian life: prayer, Bible study and memorization, service to others, and the giving of tithes, just to name a few... This is an area I had a lot of trouble with for most of my Christian life—and still do.

Sometimes the message we need to practice these disciplines walks a fine line between encouragement and guilt-inducing legalism. Or sometimes we just interpret it that way. My daily quiet times have never been daily. There are stretches when I do have a daily quiet time, but it's often interspersed with weeks when quiet times are few and far between. I once heard somebody say that no great man of God has ever had a daily time with the Lord that wasn't early in the morning. True or not, that statement has left me with a lasting sense of failure, since I'm not an early morning person. Thus I tend to engage in my quiet times when I'm at my best: late night. Apparently I am doomed to nothing beyond perhaps being a potentially satisfactory man of God at best.

So that's the tension within me. Are the disciplines a guilt-inducing, legalistic scoreboard of my efforts to "be Christian," or are they an often inconvenient but natural outflowing of my desire to spend time engaged with God? I wish it was always the latter, but sometimes it's definitely the former. If you're like me, you can really tell the difference. In legalism mode, the prayers are dry, the reading seems repetitive, and the service is forced. In engagement mode, the prayers are earnest (sometimes in the middle of the night), the reading is love-inducing, and service is a joy. The switch between the two, I have found, often lies in my willingness to be inconvenienced. When I resent it, legalism prevails. When I obey with an expectant heart, God shows up.

Back to the baggage: if I get complacent and leave the switch in the "inconvenient/I don't want to/legalism" position, discipleship halts. And that switch gets locked in the legalism position if I then convince myself that it doesn't really matter anyway, since I'm already assured of going to heaven.

But guess what? Jesus knew we'd be this way:

You did not choose Me, but I chose you.

John 15:16

He knew we wouldn't seek Him out all by ourselves. Paul observed it as well:

There is no one who understands; there is no one who seeks God. All have turned away.

Romans 3:11–12

Did you know that Jesus prayed for you on this very issue?

*I pray not only for these [the disciples with him], but also for those who believe in Me through their message. May they all be one, as You, Father, are in Me and I am in You. May they also **be one in Us,** so the world may believe You sent Me. I have given them the glory You have given Me. May they be one as We are one. **I am in them** and You are in Me.*

John 17:20–23 (emphasis added)

Was Jesus praying for the universal church? Yes, it seems so. Just prior to this prayer, He prayed for His small group of disciples; there's no reason to think He wasn't also praying for His big future group of disciples, including you and me. This passage is often cited as a call to unity within the church body, but don't miss the concept He repeats twice: may they be in Us. Complete engagement is the end result of a successful discipleship process. At that point, prayer has become more than a daily ten-minute routine, it's an ongoing process throughout every day. Bible reading is not a quick perusal of a single chapter, it's a time of anxiously awaited comfort in God's presence. Tithing is not a reluctant bank cheque given at the end of the month, it's an act of worship at the beginning of the month. As such, the disciplines are no longer individual tasks but wholly natural expressions of our very nature in Him.

Let us also not forget the work and role of the Holy Spirit in guiding us through the paths of discipleship (John 16:13). The Holy Spirit is even more help so that it's not entirely dependent on our own efforts.

So, where to start losing this luggage? Sheer willpower probably won't do it, so I can't recommend making determined resolutions for change. Whenever I'm faced with the reality that I need to push aside my feelings of inconvenience to do something I feel God calling me to do, I remember two short prayers I learned as a teenager from the director at a summer camp where I worked: "God, I am willing to be made willing" and "My only hope is You."

These aren't magic words, but they express a heart that wants to seek God but needs a push from Someone. For a more extensive overview on seeking the push (filling) of the Holy Spirit, I highly recommend *How to Be Filled with the Holy Spirit* by A.W. Tozer.[12]

An honest heart will quickly see the truth in these two prayers. I cannot always claim to be willing to do everything I know I should, but I'm willing to be made willing; more than that, I'm willing to be made wanting! My own efforts to engage in discipleship so often come up short-lived, frustrated, and quickly forgotten. I might as well acknowledge to God up front that my only hope is Him—something that probably needs to be prayed on a regular basis as we ask for the push of the Holy Spirit to help us do the things we don't always want to do.

And lastly, remember that daily engagement with God is going to seem inconvenient at times. Jesus didn't call it taking up your cross for no reason. So expect it, but don't let it stop you. And drop that thought about heaven being the only important goal of our surrender to Him. Our becoming a slave of Jesus Christ is just as much about our lives starting right now.

---

12 A.W. Tozer, *How to Be Filled with the Holy Spirit* (Harrisburg, PA: Christian Publications, 1960).

Heavenly Father,

I want to love You with all my heart, with all my soul, and with all my strength. But my heart, my soul, and my strength don't always do the things I want them to do.

When You call, sometimes I pretend I'm busy. When You speak, sometimes I pretend I can't hear.

Forgive me for readily accepting Your gift of eternal life all the while turning down Your gift of abundant life with You now.

I know the disciplines I should embrace, not out of duty but out of desire to be with You. And yet I don't do them.

Change my heart. I'm willing to be made willing. Turn my prayers into conversations, my reading into listening, and my service into cheerful gifts. Fill me with Your Holy Spirit, for my only hope is You. Amen.

Luggage Six

"I need to learn more
before God can use me."

We live in a culture addicted to experts. Everything we learn, we want to learn from an expert. Whether it's planting gardens, learning to ski, or analyzing a sports event, we want our information from the people at the forefront of knowledge and experience. Anything less just won't do.

As an endocrinologist, I get a phone call or letter about once a week from a doctor who wants me to see a patient of theirs regarding a nonexistent hormone issue. Usually the patient is convinced they have a "glandular problem," thyroid being the most common scapegoat. They believe everything that bothers them will get better if they can just get their thyroid treated. The only problem is, all their thyroid tests come back completely normal. The referring doctor is usually apologetic and says they realize the patient's thyroid is not diseased at all, but the patient is insistent that they hear it from "an expert."

Sometimes my role as a hormone expert has gotten me into some awkward situations. Once, during a day on-call at the hospital, I was asked to consult on a young woman in labour who had diabetes. As I walked into her room on the delivery ward, I recognized her husband as a longstanding patient of mine. He had a hormone condition that had required a fairly long treatment course in order to restore his fertility. I had two students with me and the room was full of nurses charting and setting up IVs. As soon as I entered the room, the husband pointed at me, and called out in a loud voice, "Hey, everyone, look! Here is the man who's responsible for this!" He was pointing at his wife's very pregnant belly. There were a few awkward moments as the students and nurses stared at me as if they had suddenly entered a real life soap opera.

"No, Jim," I replied, much to the relieved laughter of everyone in the room, "you are the man who's responsible for this. I'm just your physician!"

Indeed, we can be quite grateful for the assistance of experts, but we have also come to demand experts as a prerequisite for making big decisions or interpreting information.

Where am I going with this? Don't worry, I'm certainly not anti-education or anti-intellectual. We do need and benefit from many types of experts in our culture. That includes the church; it's critically important that our Bible colleges, seminaries, Bible studies, discipleship programs, and sermons continue to instruct and develop people, whether they're heading into full-time ministry or not. This is an important point I will emphasize again later.

What I'm getting at is not whether we need experts. It's whether we expect ourselves to become experts in theology or ministry before allowing God to take us and use us for His purposes.

How many times have you heard, or thought, something like this: "I can't be a small group leader because I don't know how to answer difficult questions about the Bible" or "I can't share my faith because I don't know enough about talking to people who believe in different worldviews." Or on an even smaller scale, "I don't want to pray aloud with people, because when I do, it comes out all stuttered and disorganized; I need to learn how to pray better first."

I can't find any place in the Bible where it says we need to learn everything *before* taking a step and entering God's service. In fact, Jesus spoke about this. It was obviously so impactful that His words on the topic made it into three gospels.

You will even be brought before governors and kings because of Me, to bear witness to them and to the nations. But when they hand you over, don't worry about how or what you should speak. For you will be given what to say at that hour, because you are not speaking, but the Spirit of your Father is speaking through you.

Matthew 10:18–20

Whenever they bring you before synagogues and rulers and author-ities, don't worry about how you should defend yourselves or what you should say. For the Holy Spirit will teach you at that very hour what must be said.

Luke 12:11–12

So when they arrest you and hand you over, don't worry beforehand what you will say. On the contrary, whatever is given to you in that hour—say it. For it isn't you speaking, but the Holy Spirit.

Mark 13:11

Is Jesus saying we don't need to worry about studying His words or delving deeper into His instructions? No! After all, He was taking His disciples through a three-year training process when He said it. But He did give them the assurance that when push came to shove, when God's name was on the line, He would provide what was necessary to accomplish His purpose.

Let me be extra clear on this: the Bible, from Jesus onwards, gives example after example of Christians being trained up, discipled, and mentored for the building up of the church. No one should assume they can decide for themselves to just *be* a leader or speaker or shepherd to God's people on the assumption that God will do all the work. We're not just inanimate puppets in His hands. Such a view would appear to be an abuse of the words and example of Jesus and the apostles.

Look again at the scenario described by Jesus. Paraphrased, He's saying, "When you're doing My work, if you're forced into a position that's beyond you, the Holy Spirit will be there to fill in the gaps."

Sometimes we might even doubt we can ever become an expert in the things of God. I've certainly felt that way reading theological texts where the author makes a point while throwing around a multitude of proof texts from all over the Bible, some of which only seem to fit when using a specific Greek nuance. It sometimes gets to the point where I skip ahead to another chapter or just close the book for good and decide I'm just never going to really understand that aspect of the Word, let alone be able to teach it to someone else.

At times when I doubt my spiritual sophistication, I like to remember one of my favourite stories of Jesus with His disciples. In Matthew 16:6–12, Jesus tells the disciples to *"beware of the yeast of the Pharisees…"* Matthew captures their thick-headed reply beautifully: "Um, we didn't bring any bread…"[13] Jesus has to spell it out:

"Why is it you don't understand that when I told you, 'Beware of the yeast of the Pharisees and Sadducees,' it wasn't about bread?" Then

---

13 Okay, I added the "Um," but I bet it was part of it!

they understood that He did not tell them to beware of the yeast in
bread, but of the teaching of the Pharisees and Sadducees.

Matthew 16:11–12

I love it. After giving what seems to be a straightforward allegorical lesson, Jesus has to dumb it right down and say, "Listen guys, the food bit was a teaching point. I'm not just randomly warning you about bad yeast!" In fairness, in the verse before this passage, the disciples were noting that they had forgotten to bring bread with them on the trip. They may well have been dulled by hunger; the Gospels have many other examples of the disciples' apparent dullness, simplicity, or lack of understanding. Through these accounts, the disciples have been presented in all their embarrassing naiveté for two thousand years of future generations to see. Yet these eleven men, dull and inexperienced as they may have been at the start, ultimately were used by God to have an impact on the whole of human civilization, in all parts of the world, in a way that continues to this day. Not bad for a bunch of guys who might well fail to hold a seminary faculty position today.

So how much more training and knowledge do you need? This is an interesting question, and it comes up in my own academic environment. The current fashion in academic medicine is the concept of continuous, 360-degree cross-evaluation. Which basically means I'm always being asked to provide written evaluations on students, residents, staff, and my colleagues, often with a sit-down discussion of the comments and/or their grades. In turn, I'm regularly evaluated by students and my peers. Once in a while, we try to see a patient or two in between all the evaluations.

One of the curious things I've noticed after years of this activity is how poorly we judge our capabilities. It seems quite rare to find an individual who really seems to know exactly where they stand. Most people, including myself, tend to over or underestimate their abilities and contributions, at least compared to the valuations of others.

And so I've come up with a general rule regarding the question of "more training." If you think you don't need any more training or knowledge, you're almost certainly overestimating your abilities and really do need some further investment in education. Conversely, if you think you do need more training and knowledge before you can do anything, you're probably underestimating your abilities and failing to put what you have to use.

There might be some interesting parallels to our lives as Christians, with one huge and important difference: for the service God asks of me now, He has already provided the necessary tools and knowledge. He's also promised to supply any urgent last-minute needs as they arise.

What's the baggage then? The very prevalent idea that God has a plan for me in the future, but I can't engage in any service to Him now, at least not until I learn more about Him. This thinking reminds me of a sign I once saw outside a pub in Ireland: "Free drinks tomorrow." Except the sign was mounted on the wall as a permanent fixture. If you go in and ask about the free drinks…well, it's always tomorrow.

I'll never learn all there is to know about God. There will always be more, which should come as no surprise, as He is infinite! But refusing to engage in His plan today is like waiting for those free drinks at the pub tomorrow. They never come.

Before wrapping up this chapter, I need to make one last point dealing with the issue of gaining knowledge of God. It's actually not the goal. Oh, and about the issue of accomplishing things in His service… that's not the goal, either. It's just a byproduct of the real goal.

Paul knew the real goal:

> *[I] consider everything to be a loss in view of the surpassing value of knowing Christ Jesus my Lord. Because of Him I have suffered the loss of all things and consider them filth, so that I may gain Christ and be found in Him…*
>
> Philippians 3:8–9

Knowing all about God—not a prerequisite for engaging in His service now. *Knowing God*, well, that's the whole point of everything.

Heavenly Father,
I fully believe You have started a good work in me and that You will be faithful to carry it on to completion. Which is a good thing, because I know there's so much more of You to know.

Forgive me for thinking I can educate myself into holiness rather than watching, listening, and talking to You for daily discipleship. Help me to thirst after You rather than thirst after knowledge.

As I seek and find You, instruct me seriously in both wisdom and experience of Your ways and Your words.

Whatever I may be at this point, whatever skills I possess, and whatever limitations I may yet have, even now, I surrender it all to Your service.

Teach me to draw upon Your resources and to trust not in my own understanding as I serve You. Let me not seek knowledge but rather seek to acknowledge You in all my ways.

Let us walk together every day, as I am Yours and You are mine. Amen.

Luggage Seven

"I am allowed to have
righteous anger."

When was the last time you met someone who was angry about nothing? Or someone who was angry yet fully admitted that their anger was irrational and unwarranted? Probably never. And that's even true for kids. I can recall many occasions when one of my young daughters was upset and angry with her sister and the issue, to my assessment, was something ridiculous, like "My foot was on the footrest first" or "She keeps staring at me with a funny look in her eyes."

My reaction was usually the same. "Are you really going to start a fight over that?"

And their response was also usually the same. "Yes."

Although it seemed foolish to me, the issue was obviously important enough to them to initiate and sustain anger, followed by some type of argument and attempt at retribution.

Anger is a natural human emotion, easily summoned and often a precursor to all kinds of nasty actions, some of which carry lifelong consequences for the giver and receiver. I can't even begin to count the number of people I've met in clinic who are unable to describe their family medical history on account of the fact that they've had no contact with the various members for decades. I don't usually ask the reason for the non-contact, but some people volunteer the information anyway. The story is usually a variation of one theme: somebody said or did something that was such an offense that it resulted in a permanent rupture of the relationship. And so the rupture persists, year after year, until nobody even cares about the fact that a relationship once existed. People simply become irrelevant to each other.

Most people who are Christ-followers of any duration are familiar with the multiple verses describing God's hesitation to become angry.

> *Yahweh is a compassionate and gracious God, slow to anger and rich in faithful love and truth...*
>
> Exodus 34:6 (God describing Himself)

> *The Lord is slow to anger and rich in faithful love, forgiving wrongdoing and rebellion.*
>
> Numbers 14:18

Interestingly, three different psalms cite these verses, almost verbatim from the original:

But You, Lord, are a compassionate and gracious God, slow to anger and rich in faithful love and truth.

Psalm 86:15

The Lord is compassionate and gracious, slow to anger and rich in faithful love.

Psalm 103:8

The Lord is gracious and compassionate, slow to anger and great in faithful love.

Psalm 145:8

And there are other repetitions:

Tear your hearts, not just your clothes, and return to the Lord your God. For He is gracious and compassionate, slow to anger, rich in faithful love, and He relents from sending disaster.

Joel 2:13

But You are a forgiving God, gracious and compassionate, slow to anger and rich in faithful love…

Nehemiah 9:17

Clearly, the Old Testament writers knew that being "slow to anger" was a critically important characteristic of God. As such, it would be easy to write a chapter pointing out our need to imitate Christ in this area. The reader really shouldn't need any kind of persuading as to the importance of being gracious and forgiving.

But that's not baggage, so that's not what I'm talking about. I want to talk about what we perceive to be righteous anger, and the way in which we can sometimes convince ourselves it's the same as general, or "understandable," anger.

The account of Jesus clearing the temple of moneychangers and thieves is the only recorded time Jesus appears to pass the boiling point:

> *In the temple complex He found people selling oxen, sheep, and doves, and He also found the money changers sitting there. After making a whip out of cords, He drove everyone out of the temple complex with their sheep and oxen. He also poured out the money changers' coins and overturned the tables. He told those who were selling doves, "Get these things out of here! Stop turning My Father's house into a marketplace!"*

John 2:14–16

Because Jesus was God, and God is always perfect and justified in His actions, many Christians have come to see this passage as an example of righteous, and therefore permissible, anger. I do not dispute this. The big question then: as followers of Jesus, are we permitted/ encouraged to demonstrate righteous anger? And since we're rarely individually faced with having to clear corrupt salesmen out of our church sanctuaries, what situations in our lives would warrant it?

Herein lies the problem, and the baggage. When was the last time you felt anger and would have readily admitted it to being anything but righteous anger? Once angry about something, will we immediately acknowledge it to be definitely *unrighteous* anger? The honest experience of my heart says no. People who are angry are angry for a reason, hence the assumption that it's righteous, and that reason is almost always a result of perceived or actual injury inflicted upon them by others. Well, that's not entirely true; people can be angry with themselves, but rarely as often or as intensely as the anger we reserve for others.

Do you see the disconnect? We readily pay lip service to the principle that anger is rarely constructive and is something to resist… except of course for righteous anger, which conveniently happens to be the only anger we personally indulge. Or so we think. We justify ourselves by pointing out Jesus' very acceptable anger at something that offended Him. "Jesus got angry!" I've heard exclaimed a number of times.

Let's look more closely at the situation that led to Jesus' righteous anger. It actually doesn't take much thinking to realize that Jesus' anger was never a response to personal injury. If it was, we might have expected to see many recorded examples of Jesus lashing out in response to imperfect or evil people who threatened or offended Him. He was regularly insulted, belittled, threatened, mocked, and hated (and still is). It was so prevalent that He even warned His disciples that they would be treated similarly (Matthew 5:11). Nowhere do we read that He got huffy or sulky. He never returned the insults. Never nursed a grudge. Now, if He did, in light of the way He was often treated, we would all have agreed that He had every right to do so! But that wasn't the kind of righteous anger He demonstrated.

Think of the many times Jesus was approached by the Pharisees and teachers of the law and asked a question that was meant to trap Him into saying something that would appear inconsistent or politically dangerous. The question from Matthew 22:17 comes to mind: *"Is it lawful to pay taxes to Caesar or not?"* The next verse says that He perceived their malice, but His response was nothing more than wise, measured words that exposed the folly of their trap. He then answered, *"Therefore give back to Caesar the things that are Caesar's, and to God the things that are God's"* (Matthew 22:21). No hatred. No violence. No ranting. No plotting of revenge.

Jesus' anger was shown in just the one instance of clearing the temple, and it was in response to a situation whereby evil affairs were being conducted under the guise of religious (God's) sanction and protection. That's a far cry from people insulting me on account of my beliefs or appearance or values. Disagreements about points of faith or Scripture? Nope, not the same. Anger about who should or shouldn't be appointed to the church elders' board? Not the same. Anger about someone who seems to be ungrateful and unloving despite my attempts to be nice? Still no. What about someone taking advantage of me in a financial situation? Still not the same.

Clearly there is such a thing as righteous anger, though, so how might we differentiate it from what might otherwise be called self-related or understandable but non-righteous anger? My suggestion: righteous anger is anger that God shares, and it's rarely directed at a specific person.

Is God angry about the existence of human trafficking in so many parts of our world? I dare say He is. Therefore, I am too. Righteous anger.

Is God angry about the children who are abused by the people who are supposed to love them? Absolutely. Therefore, I am also angry about child abuse. Righteous anger.

Is God angry about the poor man who's oppressed in spirit because of his alcohol addiction? Yes, indeed. Therefore I, too, am angry about the existence of substance abuse and the broken lives it causes.

With my focus on righteous anger, does that mean I would never get angry in any scenarios that pertain specifically to injuries done against me? No, of course not. The fact is, if someone does something that intentionally or even unintentionally hurts me, my natural reaction at some point will be anger. It's probably a denial of my human nature to think anger could ever be entirely eliminated. In fact, nowhere in the Bible does it say we must never feel anger.

Rather, the key is what happens next.

> Be angry and do not sin. Don't let the sun go down on your anger,
> and don't give the Devil an opportunity.
>
> Ephesians 4:26–27[14]

Let's look at this principle from both the righteous anger and the understandable but non-righteous anger perspectives.

Understandable but non-righteous anger: I volunteer to help with a ministry in the church, and after serving faithfully in it for six years someone comes to me with multiple sharp criticisms of what I've done and suggestions for how I can do it better, without volunteering to offer any help themselves. Will I be angry at this person? Highly probable, and pretty understandable. Does God share in my anger over this situation? Well, that's a stretch. More likely, His anger will be toward the fact that two of His children are now in a very strained relationship. Conclusion: my anger at this person isn't really righteous anger, even though it may be understandable anger.

---

14 Note that the beginning of the verse is not a command to be angry, but rather a statement of fact: when you are angry, do not sin.

Is that example too soft? Let's be real then. I'm fully aware that many of us carry incredibly deep-seated hurts that can last a lifetime. There seems to be no limit to the brutality some people willingly inflict upon others. Do such things incite anger and resentment? Of course, that is to be expected. Again, the anger is understandable. Does God share in the anger? I'm sure He does—in His deep concern for the injured person and at the level of His broken heart for a world where people intentionally try to kill each other's body and spirit.

So, in a sense, there is indeed an element of righteous anger here. As it pertains to the personal injury incurred, however, there's still no leeway for refusing individual forgiveness, even though we'll continue to share His anger at the ongoing evil and oppression in the world.

Let me pause to acknowledge that a comprehensive overview of personal healing and forgiveness towards others is beyond the scope of this book. In no way do I mean to minimize the important work (often performed with the assistance of a trained counsellor) and time required to deal with the events and people that have caused hurt in one's life. Recovery can be a difficult and slow process, and I don't mean to imply that there are anger and forgiveness switches that can be easily flipped on or off at a whim. Reconciliation can certainly take a lot of time and effort, but there's simply no biblical support to the idea that permissible, understandable anger equates with permanent non-forgiveness and the holding of grudges.

So, in conclusion, is there such thing as righteous anger? The answer is yes, but with several caveats:

1. Righteous anger is characterized by an anger at things or situations that grieve God's heart, not ours.
2. Righteous anger is not an excuse or permission to hold a grudge against a specific individual.
3. Righteous anger never justifies vengeance enacted by us, even if we think we're acting on God's behalf. (Actually, if you're thinking that you're the instrument of God's vengeance, you need to remind yourself of Romans 12:19, where it specifically says you're not!)

4. All other causes of anger are self-related anger, which is not inherently sinful provided that it's short-lived, does not lead to sin or retribution, and is quickly followed by forgiveness, whether asked for or not.

The baggage we need to drop: the misunderstanding of Jesus' actions that leads us to believe understandable anger is the same as righteous anger, and therefore permissible and permanent. This misunderstanding does exactly the opposite of what Ephesians 4:26 warns: it gives the Devil a foothold in our lives.

Before leaving this chapter, I want to reflect a bit longer on the verses that got it all started, the ones that say God is slow to anger. While I recognize that anger is a natural human emotion, I'm not sure it's therefore healthy to indulge it whenever it arises. It's interesting that when God first revealed His nature to Moses, He stressed this point: "I'm not easily angered!" Multiple subsequent Old Testament prophets and writers repeated and reminded people of that quality, surely something for us to imitate.

So, how can we become "slow to anger"? Well, if you read the Luggage Four section, you'll know my views on this one. Resolving to try harder isn't likely to be successful. Ultimately, this requires a change of heart and character, which only the Holy Spirit can accomplish within us (though we also have to be willing to change). "Work harder at something and you'll be changed" is a time-honoured formula for failure and frustration. Repentance and surrender... that's the real ticket.

How can we partner with the Holy Spirit in cultivating a character of grace rather than anger? For several years, I have meditated upon, prayed about, and asked God to help me pursue the goal of becoming "unoffendable." I hope God is using that to cause me to become slow(er) to anger.

I believe the trait of "unoffendability" is a reflection of Christ's character and is a practical demonstration of grace. Again, this doesn't mean we're unoffended by societal injustices, oppression, and any evil that enslaves humankind—such things are highly offensive—but the object of our offense is the Devil and the accompanying depravity of the natural human heart. Rather, in becoming "unoffendable," I seek to avoid taking offense at the things said and done by others to me.

How many times have you seen or experienced a situation where someone said something, often unintentionally, and another person was offended? Daily. And what's the natural response to being offended? Hurt, then anger, then bitterness. It's so often unnecessary, since the offense was never intended in the first place! People say things all the time without thinking about how their words will be heard by others. Clearly, I can't just turn off my anger at will once it starts, so being "slow to anger" will have to begin with a refusal to perceive everything as an insensitive or direct attack. Practically, in concert with prayer and regular discussions with God, what does this look like?

1. If someone says something that seems insensitive, uncaring, or hurtful to me, and I'm not sure if it was intentional, I'll choose to assume it was unintentional.

2. If someone says or does something that seems harsh or insulting to me and it is clearly intentional, I'll choose to assume they are acting out of anger and hurt themselves, and thus their actions are reflections of their own hurt and not out of true hate for me.

3. Quite often, I recognize that the assumptions of the second point will be wrong. Some people may indeed act out of actual hate towards me. In these situations, it's important to meet with the person to discuss the issue—perhaps to make sure the whole thing didn't arise as a response to some action towards them for which I need to ask forgiveness! Regardless of their attitude and the outcome of any such discussions, this is where I'll specifically choose to be unoffended, refusing to become a partner in mutual hate.

Am I now an expert in unoffendability? Nope![15] But I've found this to be a practical approach to turning the other cheek. It's one of two char-

---

15 See the concluding section for a full disclosure of my hypocrisy in writing about that which I have not mastered myself.

acter goals I'm asking God to write upon my life as a tangible transformation to His likeness. I'll talk about the other one later.

A number of my closest friends know about my unoffendability goal, and they have adopted it as well. I have to say, it has led to the most incredible freedom in relationship. We're now entirely secure in our knowledge of our brotherly love for one another. We need not fear saying the wrong thing or being misunderstood since each of us knows any offense which may occur will be unintentional and always be met with quiet grace and subsequent forgetting of the event. I have no fear of ever losing such friends.

What kind of transformation would occur in all of our lives if everyone practiced this? What would it do for families if each irritation and insult was met with nothing but grace because the recipient chose to be unoffended by focussing on the known, shared love instead of the momentary attack? It literally brings tears to my ears to think of the limitless reconciliation that would suddenly appear.

Righteous anger? Always, but only in concert with God's concern for justice and never directed at specific individuals or people groups. Remember Romans 2:4—

... do you despise the riches of His kindness, restraint, and patience, not recognizing that God's kindness is intended to lead [them] to repentance?

You may notice I changed "you" to "them," to better reflect the tone of the surrounding passage in Romans. God has a reason to act with restraint in the face of evil—to lead us all to repentance. How then dare we do otherwise?

What about understandable anger arising from things that specific people do to me? Less and less and less and less. Grace is so much better.

Heavenly Father,

Your mercies are new every morning. You are a faithful God who keeps His gracious covenant for a thousand generations with those who love You and keep Your commands. You are slow to anger and rich in faithful love, forgiving my wrongdoing and re-bellion.

How much I want to be like You! And yet I am not. I can be so easily goaded into annoyance, irritation, and anger. And the things that follow can be so displeasing to You.

Forgive me for the times when I return hurt for hurt, and in doing so dishonour the name of the One I claim to follow.

Remove any such footholds the Devil may think he has in my life. Break my heart for what breaks Yours, but steel my heart against my natural reactions to personal injury.

In doing so, transform my character into one Heavenly word: grace. Amen.

Luggage Eight

"As a Christian, God expects me to show boldness and
courage by defending Him and His interests."

I have such fond memories of my childhood church. A couple weeks ago, I attended one of my daughter's school Easter concerts, which was held in a nearby church. It was done in collaboration with the school alumni adult choir, complete with orchestra, men's quartet, and ladies' trio. They performed a musical of the style that was so popular in the 70s and 80s—a medley of grand hymns interspersed with a deep-voiced narrator quoting Scripture and proclaiming the good news over the rumble of tympani and heralds of trombones. My wife was wondering why I had such a goofy grin on my face the whole time; I was certainly enjoying it, and the quality of the production was great, but the grin was because it reminded me so vividly of my childhood church and the grand musicals we used to present at major holidays. We had some wonderfully gifted music pastors. I can't speak for every church, but it seems that the Christian musical has fallen out of fashion these days, perhaps for better, perhaps for worse. Who knows? Over the years, so many things have changed in our Western evangelical churches. Sometimes I do miss that old stuff!

However, one thing I don't miss: the singing of Christian war songs. I remember standing in the packed sanctuary hearing the congregation belt out "Onward Christian soldiers, marching as to war!" and "Stand up, stand up for Jesus, ye soldiers of the cross, lift high His royal banner, it must not suffer loss!"

Perhaps it's my liberally educated post-modern cultural mindset misinterpreting the events and motives of the past, as the liberally educated post-modern cultural mindset is wont to do, but the thought of singing/shouting those verses in church now makes me cringe. I certainly recognize that those verses were written in a different time and in a different type of war-influenced culture and may not have been intended to reflect a desire for violent imposition of Christianity upon the world, even though it sounds like it. In fact, interpreted in the context of spiritual warfare, such lines are completely understandable and even biblical.

According to the story of the "Stand Up for Jesus" hymn as reported at www.sharefaith.com, the preacher who inspired it was a godly man known for speaking out against oppression. The warfare envisioned was war against slavery, not war against a people group. In that light, it's a worthy set of verses. Perhaps it's a tragedy that the real stories and sentiments behind many old hymns are completely unknown to many Christians today. So, if any of my readers are lovers of the old hymns, don't be offended. "Crown Him with Many Crowns" still gives me chills the odd time our church sings it. It's usually done to appease the old folks, which now includes me.

I wonder if we really do interpret such lines and attitudes in a spiritual sense, or whether there just might be some baggage that's emerged in the modern understanding of "Stand Up for Jesus." Without question, there are clear biblical instructions that we should never be ashamed of our faith in Christ. More than that, we shouldn't hesitate to identify ourselves publicly with Him and His church.

Therefore, everyone who will acknowledge Me before men, I will also acknowledge him before My Father in heaven.

Matthew 10:32

And I say to you, anyone who acknowledges Me before men, the Son of Man will also acknowledge him before the angels of God, but whoever denies Me before men will be denied before the angels of God.

Luke 12:8–9

You are the salt of the earth. But if the salt should lose its taste, how can it be made salty? It's no longer good for anything but to be thrown out and trampled on by men. You are the light of the world. A city situated on a hill cannot be hidden. No one lights a lamp and puts it under a basket, but rather on a lampstand, and it gives light for all who are in the house. In the same way, let your light shine before men, so that they may see your good works and give glory to your Father in heaven.

Matthew 5:13–16

For I am not ashamed of the gospel, because it is God's power for salvation to everyone who believes, first to the Jew, and also to the Greek.

Romans 1:16

On top of this, the whole practice of baptism is commonly understood to be a tangible, public declaration of faith and identification with Christ, notwithstanding unfortunate controversies that have split the church over the years on this point.

So, is there a difference between "acknowledging Him before men" and "standing up for Jesus"? Perhaps not in the minds of the New Testament writers and many Christians, and that's fine. But in our culture and language, I wonder if there actually is a subtle difference in the way we practically live out those instructions. I wonder if our actions are always in keeping with Scripture's intent.

In today's world, what exactly does it mean to stand up for Jesus? Seriously, beyond being a general mindset and avoiding the overt denial of faith, what specific actions are expected by this exhortation?

My observation of Christianity in the world suggests to me that "standing up for Jesus" appears to fall into one of two separate categories of actions. One: hard work by Christ-followers to bring mercy and grace, openly inspired by Christ, into the midst of darkness and brokenness around the world in the hopes of being instruments of His kindness that leads people to repentance (see Romans 2:4 again). Two: belligerence and stubborn, prideful belief, often mixed with a healthy dose of culture and politics, with the stated intent of imposing a Christian moral code upon those who don't yet even know Jesus. Ouch.

Maybe I should end this chapter right here. Who appointed me as judge over my Christian brothers and sisters? Nobody. And believe me, I'm not picturing any particular person as I write this; if anything, I must inspect my own actions with my non-Christian friends and colleagues to see if I can figure out which category they would put me in if asked about my own expression of faith.

Am I arguing against Christian involvement in public life and the decisions of the nation? Of course not. If we are true Christ-followers, His character and God's law must be indelibly written upon our hearts and thus reflected in our character and actions. The question is, what facet will be the best reflection of Christ to a world that doesn't even know their own needs—His law or His life?

Strictly and solely reflecting His law (i.e. rules) effectively looks like me telling other people what to do. Most likely what they hear from that approach is "Be like me, cuz I'm doing it right." In a pluralistic and relativistic world, the practice of preaching rules without preaching the life and gift of Christ's love would appear to be nothing more than bullying. Subsequently adding "These rules are right because the Bible says so" then carries the appearance of cultural imperialism of the worst kind. Not to mention, that phrase misses the whole point of God's gift of salvation, which is freedom in Christ!

Let's face it. Even if the nation decided, in some inexplicable way, to adopt Christian morality as the backbone for all legislation and life, that alone wouldn't result in a single additional soul finding life in Christ. No amount of biblical living without Christ can produce life transformation or salvation. If someone who has yet to meet Jesus observes my life and sees nothing but a stricter set of rules for living compared to their own, they have completely missed (or I have failed to show) everything that's beautiful and life-giving about following Him.

To be sure, living one's life according to principles that directly contradict God's law can bring serious and tragic consequences, a point that really doesn't need to be argued here. But the point of the law is to show us how much we need Christ (Romans 3:20, 28— *"For no one will be justified in His sight by the works of the law, because the knowledge of sin comes through the law... For we conclude that a man is justified by faith apart from the works of the law"*). It's not just a recipe book for an orderly life. Wielded by man as a code for legislation, it's nothing more than a tool for oppression (see Matthew 23:23, 27— *"Woe to you, scribes and Pharisees, hypocrites! You pay a tenth of mint, dill, and cumin, yet you have neglected the more important matters of the law—justice, mercy, and faith... You are like whitewashed tombs, which appear beautiful on the outside, but inside are full of dead men's bones and every impurity"*), something the church has tragically demonstrated time and time again over the course of history.

Let's bring this discussion back to practicality. Many Christians I've met would indeed be ashamed of events/movements in the past that have fallen into the second "stand up for Jesus" category. Thus it would be pretty easy to say this chapter is really just a rant against the cultural and political overflows of some branches of the church. But I wonder if our baggage actually goes deeper and to a much subtler holding area than we think.

Here's what I mean. There's no greater hero in our society than the self-made man or woman. Everyone loves the rags-to-riches story, the Cinderella story. How many times as kids were we told "You can do it!" or "You can do anything if you just put your mind to it!"? This goes perfectly with our current cultural obsession of instilling overabundant self-confidence in our children and teenagers. And when faced with adversity or anything that stands in our way, what do we do? Stand up for ourselves, of course.

In fairness, let's not hang this entirely on the current generation. Remember that Frank Sinatra confidently sang, "I did it *my way.*" To be sure, there's some value in self-assertion, but when it's phrased in such antagonistic terms, the accompanying emotion is often contempt for anyone who's perceived as getting in the way or being in non-agreement.

Herein lies the real baggage of "standing up for Jesus." Do I have contempt for the person whose words/actions seem to display disrespect for God? Even worse, do I secretly harbour glee that one day such a person will have to answer to God for their deeds? Do I wash my hands of them, deciding in advance and on God's behalf that they're a lost cause?

If so, that baggage puts me in direct opposition to God's own heart:

> But I tell you, love your enemies and pray for those who persecute you, so that you may be sons of your Father in heaven. For He causes His sun to rise on the evil and the good, and sends rain on the righteous and the unrighteous.
>
> Matthew 5:44–45

> The Lord does not delay His promise, as some understand delay, but is patient with you, not wanting any to perish but all to come to repentance.
>
> 2 Peter 3:9

> I tell you, in the same way, there is joy in the presence of God's angels over one sinner who repents.
>
> Luke 15:10

As can be seen, the second "stand up for Jesus" category is easily recognized when a self-described Christian rants or spews hate against a "heathen" in the news. This makes us all cringe, but a similar attitude in our hearts may not be as rare as one might think.

This is the baggage that needs to be dropped: *any attitude except compassion for those who are openly opposed to Jesus and His church.* Quiet contempt or anxiously anticipating the judgement of another person is hardly a reflection of Jesus' character or His persistent love for even those who hate Him.

Someday, those who hate God will pay a steep price for their rebellion, and in general we can all look forward to the day when God finally puts a permanent stop to the evil that plagues this world. However, until then, in keeping with God's own desires, we must hold out hope that those currently in rebellion will eventually surrender to Jesus and be transformed into a new creation. Thankfully for all of us, God has always been in the business of rescuing scoundrels and remaking them as His children. What a privilege it is to be part of any such salvation story! All the more reason to throw away contempt or disdain for the non-believer and replace it with compassion, concern, and words that introduce Jesus to those who need Him so badly.

A good friend of mine has a career in a Christian non-governmental organization, bringing tangible relief and care to some of the darkest parts of the world. Once, when he was being interviewed on a local radio show, the host marvelled at my friend's persistence in going to places where he was often not wanted, where he was directly opposed and occasionally in danger of losing his life. "Why do you do these things?" he was asked. His reply: "The love of Christ compels me to do so."

That's standing up for Jesus. Lift high His royal banner; it will not suffer loss.

Heavenly Father,
Yours is the name above all names, but not everyone acknowledges it as such.

I take delight in knowing that some who now hate You will yet be transformed by the complete renewing of their minds and the opening of their eyes. Though they don't know You yet, You love them as much as You ever will. And as much as You love me now.

May I always be of the same mind as You. When people mock and profane Your name, may I respond with compassion. In standing up for You, help me remember that without You, I do not stand at all.

May my life be an accurate reflection of You and be used by You to bring many sons to glory. Amen.

Luggage Nine

"It's my responsibility to find
and attend a good church."

By this point, you've surely noticed that each luggage section begins with a statement that actually looks correct upon first glance. This section is no exception, for indeed it is our responsibility to belong to a local church/body of fellow Christ-followers. How can this be considered a piece of luggage to be dropped?

Let me start with a sheepish confession. Writing this book has me wrestling with whether I appear to others as "holier than thou." Hopefully not. That's not my heart, but I'm deeply worried about coming across that way. Maybe a little confessional writing will be a good tonic.

I left my childhood church when I started university. I didn't leave my faith (it certainly got challenged during that time), but I did leave my church. At the time, I told myself it was a good decision because I wanted to go somewhere with more "modern" worship—you know, like with overhead projectors that displayed messily written choruses, where the instruments needed to be plugged in, where the drummer was so rocking that they needed a plastic screen to keep from blowing the rest of the worship band off the stage. The worship songs at my new church would be "more real," "more worshipful," something I could "get into" as opposed to the old-school, hippie-inspired songs like "They'll know we are Christians by our love." I wanted a speaker who was cool, who could speak to me about the reality of the world and other "real" topics, who was funny and full of amazing stories. I didn't want to sit in a wooden pew and listen to some boring chapter-by-chapter biblical expository teaching from a pastor with serious seminary credentials. I wanted to be in a place that was crowded—really crowded—with lots of people all joining in. I wanted to be with people who were like me—young, energetic, and ambitious. I didn't want to be around people who had known me as a child, out of my completely ungrounded assumption that they would continue to treat me as a child.

Oh yes, and girls. I wanted to meet some hot Christian chicks. The girls from my old youth group were too much like sisters to be considered for dating.

So I left. As did many of my childhood church friends. In doing so, we effectively robbed our home church of its next generation of servants and leaders. Ultimately, many of us left town for school or work and so would have left anyway, but the point remains.

Now, there was nothing wrong with my new church; it certainly wasn't the fault of its people that I chose to go there. But when I look back at that time of my life, I'm not sure I really "joined" that church in a biblical fashion. I'll come back to this point in a few moments.

Ultimately, I did meet my hot Christian chick. We got married, had kids, and now attend a church near our home. In a true display of hypocrisy, I now find myself terribly upset at the thought that our kids and their friends might one day leave our church to go somewhere else.

At this stage, the reader might well think I'm about to launch into a chapter decrying the modern "church hopper," the person who goes from church to church, always finding fault, always looking for something better. Perhaps I am, a little bit, but only to make the point that this behaviour is seen in people who by all other outward accounts would seem to be serious Christ-followers. It's not just the "seekers." In fact, I'd argue the seekers are sometimes more loyal to a local church than some of the more typical "church people."

I'm going to stop there. Other authors, speakers, and pastors have written or spoken extensively on the rise of consumerism in the modern church. It's a pretty easy target. As before, I want to look deeper at the matter, to challenge some baggage we might not even know we own.

What does it mean to belong to a church? Does it mean we show up for Sunday services? Well, yes, that's surely part of it:

[Let us not be] staying away from our worship meetings, as some habitually do, but encouraging each other…

Hebrews 10:25

Does it mean we get to know the pastors on a first-name basis? Sure, I guess, although there are some ways of getting the pastor to know your name that are maybe less edifying… such as by sending weekly emails critiquing the sermons.

Does it mean we serve in the church? Again, to some extent this is true, since we are to serve one another and God has indeed given various gifts to the different members of His church in order to make up a complete body (1 Corinthians 12:27—*"Now you are the body of Christ, and individual members of it"*).

It's been my observation that it's all too easy to serve in the church without ever becoming truly participatory. I know it because I've done it. I once attended a mega church where there were so many people that it seemed hard to know what, if any, service needs even existed. As such, I was mostly just one more face in the crowd. I would have been happy to serve; there just didn't seem to be any obvious needs. At least, no one asked me.[16]

My wife, on the other hand, is exceptionally gifted with children and teaching, so she was right in there with the children's ministry. She did a great job and took leadership responsibilities on a regular basis. Lacking anything else to contribute, I often joined in as a children's church worker, although I may well have left it out of my Christian credentials. It's just as well; although I love my own children dearly, it's a profound understatement to say that working with toddlers doesn't align with my gifts. I might prefer to clean the church toilets; no offense to those who really do this as their act of service. Was I friendly? Of course. Did I make efforts to play with the kids? Yes. But did I engage with the kids and get to know them as individuals? Not really. I was counting the minutes until the service ended. Did I ever engage the parents who dropped off and picked up? No. Mostly, I secretly groused about how some of them never seemed to take their turn in the nursery. After a year, I remarked to Shannon that after all that time in the children's ministry, I hadn't met a single new person and my involvement had never extended beyond 6:30 to 8:00 p.m. at the Saturday night service. It was sacrificial service, right? Well, sort of, but not really—more like a conscripted tour of duty.

Don't misunderstand me. There are many occasions in church life when we're called upon to give sacrificially of our time, to do jobs that don't interest us, to pick up tasks when no one else will. Done with a cheerful heart, those tasks are necessary and will be pleasing to God. My

---

16 "We should always wait to be asked to help instead of volunteering" might be a luggage section for a future book!

point is that it's possible to serve in the church without really participating in the true life of the church. Paul knew this and seemed to single out church choir members as particular offenders:

> *If I speak angelic languages but do not have love, I am a sounding gong or a clanging cymbal.*
>
> 1 Corinthians 13:1

Just kidding, but you get the point. Service in and of itself isn't what God has in mind for the church.

So, beyond showing up on Sundays and serving in the ministries, what does it mean to truly belong to the church? I suspect most of us would look to the early church described in Acts 2:41–47 for the answer.

Every couple of years, some church somewhere gets touted as being an up-and-coming "New Testament" church. This is held up as the ideal. People flock to this church... for a while. What does it mean to be a New Testament church? Again, it's well beyond my scope and expertise to write a comprehensive overview of the early church, but the face-value description is pretty remarkable. Three thousand people joined in one day. They were devoted to learning about God, and to fellowship and prayer. Signs and wonders occurred, and there was commonality of possessions, shared meals, and daily temple meetings. These people were humble, full of joy, and found favour with all the people. Not surprisingly, new people joined the church every day. Sounds great, and I'm sure every serious Christian would love to see this in action in modern times.

At the risk of seeming like a terrible cynic, I wonder how many of our New-Testament-modelled churches today actually match the historical New Testament church. Without any bitterness or condescension in my heart towards churches that try to replicate this, I wonder if we sometimes judge a church to be New Testament purely according to its rank on the excitement scale: people were excited in the New Testament church, therefore if people are excited about a church, it's a New Testament church. Let's broaden the scope: I wonder if we judge all churches according to their excitement scale. I wonder if we *choose* our churches based on excitement.

There's nothing wrong with excitement in a church. In fact, it's a good thing. Everything seems to run better when people are excited. Programs are more attractive when people are excited. The pastor seems more good-looking and respected when people are excited. Volunteerism skyrockets when people are excited about what's happening in the church. Even books get taken out of the church library when people are excited. All good.

Notice that the church of Acts 2 wasn't just defined by excitement and fervour, although that was definitely part of it. They were devoted to living out the mission of Christ (the apostles' teachings) on a daily basis. They spent time with each other (fellowship). Daily, not just Sundays during the school year. They met each other's needs (commonality of possessions). Daily, not just in response to a fundraising campaign. They prayed for the church and devoted themselves to corporate prayer. Daily, not just when someone got cancer.

Not surprisingly, the church grew.

There seems to be no mention of people wandering about, looking to see which church had the best pastor, who had the worship style that matched the music on their iPod, who had a kids program so cool it almost guaranteed the kids would never question their faith. They just belonged to each other and to God.

What does it mean to belong to a church? The Bible demonstrates that it simply means seeking God and living with each other.

Isn't it interesting how many church groups come and go? Accountability groups, small groups, men's groups, women's groups, discipleship groups, prayer groups, study groups, support groups, young moms groups, businessmen groups, church travel groups, Christian weight loss groups, and so on. These are all good ideas, and many wonderful things have come out of such groups.

It's easy to see why these fads come, but why do they go? I suggest that it's because many of these groups attempt, but with limited success, to push us to do what we should be doing anyway—living with each other, praying with each other, praying for each other, and giving to each other—all spontaneously, not out of compulsion. This is what it means to join a church. It's so much more than just attendance and service. Unfortunately, one can never assess the health and life of a church according to the experience of a Sunday service. This makes choosing a church according to worship style akin to buying a car according to paint colour. You have no idea what's under the hood.

Of all the chapters thus far, this one makes me feel the most hypocritical and ashamed. After forty-plus years of attending church, how many of them were spent living out actual, biblical church behaviour? So few. The baggage of believing that my regular church attendance qualifies as participation in church life is one I desperately need to drop, but I hang on because it's so comfortable to keep things the way they are.

Attending Sunday services? Yes, easy. Serving according to my gifts and where needed? Yes. Perhaps occasionally sacrificial, but overall it's not too hard. Living with, praying for, and loving the people of my church on a daily basis? Help us, Jesus.

Heavenly Father,

I glibly quote the words "The church is Your bride." So commonly I treat her like my personal slave. Three thousand people joining our church in one day seems a bigger miracle today than walking on water, in light of the way we conduct ourselves in the church some days. In light of the way I conduct myself in the church some days.

For serving without love, please forgive me, and for the self-righteous attitude that comes with my self-admiration of my supposed sacrificial service.

Use me to start a new work in Your local church. Teach me to see the people as having been given to me for their own well-being and care, just as I learn to be given to them for the care and fellowship You give us all.

Let our church belong to each other as we belong to You. Cover our collective failures, that we not bring shame to You in our community. And let more and more be added to our numbers every day, starting with me. Amen.

Luggage Ten

"It's my job to help keep my fellow Christians
on the straight and narrow."

Being a pastor has got to be one of the toughest jobs there is. I sometimes think I'd like to be a pastor—until I spend some time with my buddy who's a pastor and realize I probably don't have what it takes to put up with the abuse. I don't think it was always that way. In years past, pastors were beloved and respected for their wisdom and advice.

I remember my grandparents' pastor at their Lutheran church in small-town Pennsylvania. He was a huge man who probably could have been an NFL offensive lineman. He had a jolly personality, deep belly laugh, and handshake that just about broke your wrist. His traditional Lutheran robes were probably wide enough to hide a small horse, and although we only saw him once a year at the Christmas service, he always knew our names and remarked on how big we were getting. He pastored that church for several generations and never seemed unenthusiastic— even when his congregation grew older, quieter, and sparser. One thing I'll never forget, besides my incredulity that he would stick with a dying church, was the respect I always saw in the eyes of my grandparents and the other parishioners as they shook hands with him after the service. My grandma, in particular, always wanted to show us to the pastor. Why? Because she respected him. It was meaningful for her to have such an important person compliment her on her lovely grandkids. I never heard a bad word spoken about the man.

Today things are a little different. We live in a more egalitarian society where all authority figures, pastors included, are fair game for derision and critique. In fact, pastors might get it the worst. It's their job to stand up front and tell us how to live, and many of us figure that means it's equally our job to help tell them how to live—or better yet, tell them how to tell us how to live.

I've joked that my pastor buddy could write a tell-all book when he retires, and it would probably be a bestseller. He receives so many email, letters, and phone calls from people telling him what to do. Of course, he's always been professional and never shows me letters that weren't already posted online for all to see. Today, even personal criticisms aren't private anymore. I recently heard that many pastors need to change their phone numbers and emails every six to twelve months because people don't know when to lay off with the critiques and demands.

Again, there's a nugget of truth in this chapter's baggage statement—everyone seems to be familiar with the "iron sharpens iron" proverb (see Proverbs 27:17). Thankfully, that's not the only verse we have dealing with the protocol and procedures for keeping each other accountable. Iron may sharpen iron, but have you ever listened to what that sounds like? It's nothing you want to hear on a regular basis.

But speaking the truth in love, let us grow in every way into Him who is the head—Christ.

Ephesians 4:15

Brothers, if someone is caught in any wrongdoing, you who are spiritual should restore such a person with a gentle spirit, watching out for yourselves so you also won't be tempted.

Galatians 6:1

If your brother sins against you, go and rebuke him in private. If he listens to you, you have won your brother.

Matthew 18:15

Why do you look at the speck in your brother's eye but don't notice the log in your own eye? Or how can you say to your brother, "Let me take the speck out of your eye," and look, there's a log in your eye? Hypocrite! First take the log out of your eye, and then you will see clearly to take the speck out of your brother's eye.

Matthew 7:3–5

As you can see, there are two sides to this. Clearly, we have a biblical responsibility to encourage and correct one another. But notice the operative words: privately, gently, lovingly, and humbly. You almost get the picture of someone confronting a brother with pained humility, as though they can barely stand to have to do so. At the first words of the erring brother acknowledging his wrong, the confronter interrupts with an outpouring of forgiveness and reconciliation so fast and overwhelming that the sinning brother can't even complete his apology. No baggage there!

The flip side is where the baggage lies. Rather than a feeling of loving awkwardness at the mention of error, we proudly feel we're doing our spiritual duty when rooting out even the tiniest weed with one fell swoop of St. Paul's golden sword. Again, perhaps I'm going after the low-hanging fruit. It's easy to say that apart from a few well-known exceptions in the church, most people thankfully don't seek to hunt down and slay their own pastor.

However, I fear we all carry the baggage of private judgment and condemnation from time to time. Here's an interesting exercise. Try to count the number of times in a day you've privately judged someone for something they were doing. This includes condescending thoughts, disgust, stereotyping, exasperation, feeling superior, and thinking "That's so stupid." For me, this exercise can't go on a whole day before it becomes apparent that this isn't a rare occurrence. The sad part is how often such thoughts turn into words, usually shared with a like-minded individual for our mutual, judgemental enjoyment.

The Bible is crystal clear on this point.

Do not judge, so that you won't be judged. For with the judgment you use, you will be judged, and with the measure you use, it will be measured to you.

Matthew 7:1–2

Therefore, any one of you who judges is without excuse. For when you judge another, you condemn yourself, since you, the judge, do the same things.

Romans 2:1

But you, why do you criticize your brother? Or you, why do you look down on your brother? For we will all stand before the tribunal of God.

Romans 14:10

Why this prohibition against judging others? It's simple. Judging others is an outward manifestation of pride. We usurp God's place as the judge and implementer of justice in this world, inserting ourselves in His place.

Notice the huge difference between discernment and judging. We're absolutely expected to learn to discern right from wrong, to recognize evil and flee from it.

> *Flee from youthful passions, and pursue righteousness, faith, love, and peace, along with those who call on the Lord from a pure heart. But reject foolish and ignorant disputes, knowing that they breed quarrels. The Lord's slave must not quarrel, but must be gentle to everyone, able to teach, and patient, instructing his opponents with gentleness. Perhaps God will grant them repentance leading them to the knowledge of the truth.*
>
> 2 Timothy 2:22–25

We can discern that another's actions are wrong, but we are never given the right to judge and condemn. Let me be clear: there is a scripturally prescribed process by which a continually erring believer may be gently confronted by the appropriately chosen and humble fellow believer. But personal judgement levelled in advance is not part of the procedure. Not at any time.

In order to lose this baggage, we also need to throw out its matching handbag: judging others not just according to moral principles but the irrelevant choices of everyday life that go against the advice we might give, if asked:

"I can't believe they bought that car. They don't need it."
"She really should make more of an effort to spend time with her mother."
"They ought to volunteer to do it once."
"He shouldn't just assume that he can take that coaching position."
"They really need to educate themselves a bit better about that."
"She shouldn't be going out with him."

These are all examples of judging one another, and Jesus simply said, "Don't do it." It's not a characteristic that belongs in the life of a Christ-follower. But it's so hard, isn't it? In this final chapter, I feel that I've really crossed the line; I'm calling for changes that are truly impossible. Who of us can expunge this superiority and pride from our hearts? None of us. And that's the whole point of losing the luggage—if it was purely a matter of will power, some of us might actually have accomplished it by now. Even Paul recognized he wasn't yet the person God was making him to become:

> *Brothers, I do not consider myself to have taken hold of it. But one thing I do: Forgetting what is behind and reaching forward to what is ahead...*
>
> Philippians 3:13

Besides throwing ourselves upon God's mercy for the-ever present selfish pride we carry, what can be done about this? At the risk of being repetitive, I cling to my scriptural position that we cannot just "decide" to not do this anymore. Drumming up the will to abandon judgmental attitudes will be as successful as my new year's resolution to run three miles every day, after never having done so before.

This is the second character goal I'm asking God to write upon my life. Using the model of surrendering myself to God's ability to change my character from within, I think about two things:

1. The practice of looking in my own eye, as Jesus put it. Before criticizing, confronting, or instructing another, I must ask: Am I guilty of the very same thing, maybe in a different way? When tempted to judge, can I follow Jesus' advice and see if I should firstly judge myself for an identical failure?
2. Meditate regularly upon the idea that I have no right to get upset when other people don't do what I think they should.

People will usually do what they think is best in their opinion. I may not agree, and at times I may provide solicited or unsolicited counsel. But if their final choice is something with which I don't agree, I need to ask God to teach me to respond with quiet grace and recognize that it was never my right to judge in the first place. *For all I know, they may be showing me an equal measure of grace regarding something I'm doing that they think is wrong.*

I saved this chapter for last, having added it upon the advice of my former youth pastor, who has spent thirty years in youth and family ministry. When I first told him about this book, I'd barely finished when he suggested that I needed a chapter that encouraged people to stop judging each other. Interesting indictment, isn't it? After thirty years in ministry, the number one piece of baggage he sees among Christians is our insistence upon thinking and sometimes telling each other what to do. And we wonder why we're so often offended.

Inspiring each other, or even attempting to outdo one another in honourable behaviour? Yes. Occasionally, painfully, and humbly taking someone aside to help them see a destructive pattern in their life? Yes, after much self-examination and prayerful consideration as to whether we are the right person to do so. Judging and condemning one another on a daily basis for even mundane things? Baggage.

Heavenly Father,
Without You, I can do nothing, especially not change myself. Forgive me for my dogged determination to assert my will upon others, which serves only to demonstrate the insuppressible selfish pride in my heart.

I want to live in peace with all Your children, but my own heart stands in the way of it. Yet with You, all things are possible, and by "all things," that includes impossible things.

So I surrender this heart that loves to judge. Re-create it as a heart that loves to show patience, grace, understanding, compassion, sympathy, selflessness, humility, meekness, mercy, faithfulness, joy, and love. Anything else is counterfeit and fraud, and I want it not.

Set my mind on the things above and fix my eye on what lies ahead. Help me run this race with excellence, for the prize of You. Amen.

Conclusion

Staying Away from the
Lost Luggage Room

I rarely read anything of spiritual or biblical content online, mostly because it's often impossible to know the source, worldview, qualifications, or theological bent of writers and bloggers. Articles that seem good can suddenly take a very weird twist, leaving me to wonder if the author even knows Jesus at all.

Then there are the critiques. I recognize that third-party criticisms, chatrooms, and comment blogs are the ways in which information is filtered these days. In my own scientific field, the process of peer review is a critical, if flawed, means to improve any person's submitted work.

But it's the bombastic, over the top, take-no-prisoners approach to criticism that really twists my guts into knots. Unfortunately, this technique is occasionally employed online by writers who identify as Christ-followers. It boggles my mind to read these brothers and sisters in Christ writing about how certain mainstream translations of the Bible are "satanic" or how certain established and growing evangelical denominations are leading their congregations straight into hell. Straight into hell? Really? They might want to check out Romans 8:35 (*"Who can separate us from the love of Christ?"*) The use of character assassination, absolutism, and pure hate… in the name of Jesus? Very, very sad.

Sure, I'll cringe if/when I get criticized or accused of some sort of blasphemy or mistreatment of Scripture, but hurtful comments are already part of a physician's life (just look at all those doctor rating sites) and one learns to ignore anonymous personal attacks. See my earlier comments on choosing to be unoffended. My biggest concern isn't the anonymous or unknown people's critiques, but those of people who actually know me.

For fifteen years now, I've had the privilege of lecturing and teaching in my university medical school. One of the most important teaching lessons I learned early on is this: don't bluff if you don't know something. No matter how many years of experience you have in a certain field, I guarantee that when you stand in front of 150 intelligent people who, new to the subject, see things from different perspectives, you'll be asked a question or two you've never heard before. It happens to me every single year. If you don't know the answer to a question and try to waffle, deflect, or speculate… you'll lose. The worst thing you can do is sidestep the question by asking the student an unanswerable or philosophical question in return. That just cements your status as a pretender. The student then gets a look on their face that tells you they know you don't know. Sort of a mixture of pity and contempt. It's not a nice look. It feels like you've been caught in a lie: posing as a teacher when you yourself still need to be taught.

That's my fear with this book. It's fine and dandy to write about dropping this baggage or that habit when you're a nameless, faceless writer. But there's a high risk that someone I know will read this—a family member, a friend, a colleague, or one of my patients—and upon reading it rightfully think, *He's got a lot of nerve writing about that particular issue. I saw him behave that way just last week!*

There's the rub. I'm at risk of being knee-deep in hypocrisy, and thus I'm going to follow my own advice: don't bluff. I'll own it. I have not permanently lost all ten pieces of baggage I've written about in this book. I've definitely made attempts to put them down, by praying for change, but I keep returning to the baggage claim area to pick them up again.

There are the limiting factors. I sometimes pretend I don't actually own one bag or another, then sneak back to reclaim each bag as it suits me. The lesson I've learned is that sanctification, the process of life transformation through the Holy Spirit, is a process. It's a work that is performed by the Spirit over time, but it's definitely accelerated or blocked according to my level of cooperation. I wonder if that message is widely understood in our churches; I don't think I came to understand this until recently.

I laugh at myself when I think about my process for choosing our small group study topics. I'll pour over multiple study options and frequently dismiss some of them with the thought, *We can't study that again;*

we did a similar study three years ago. As if we remember all the lessons exactly and have implemented them to perfection! How do pastors manage to continually find "new" stuff to preach about? Is it even fair or right that we expect them to do so? Sanctification isn't like medical school. In med school, you get one lecture on each topic. That's it. But it's the student's responsibility to know it and practice it, correctly and permanently. There's no time for giving the same lecture twice.

Surrendering to God's transformation is the opposite of this, at least in my life. I need to be reminded to surrender repeatedly. I need to be told to drop the baggage over and over and over again, and to remember that dropping the baggage doesn't accomplish anything in and of itself; it's just a process of removing the obstructions to God's work that I have built along the way.

So, what will I do with this book? Even though I wrote it, I plan on reading and rereading it, if for no other reason than to be reminded of the attitudinal changes needed and to pray the prayers of surrender over and over again. I cannot be satisfied with a single, momentary experience of surrender; it must become my daily focus. Just think what it will look like when I finally drop all this luggage.

Surrendering my life to Him will be the smartest move I ever choose when planning my life. The resources He gives me will be used selflessly to expand His Kingdom. God will use the circumstances and choices of my life to ultimately fulfill His Will. Becoming like Jesus will progress through God's power, changing me from within. While I look forward to being with Him in heaven one day, I will delight in our relationship today. With time, I will learn more about God, but I'll offer my life for His works even now.

I will become slow to anger, just like God. I will stand up for Jesus by allowing myself to be used by God as an instrument of His kindness and patience with the world. I will give myself to the fellowship and service of my brothers and sisters in the church God has assembled. I will flee from evil, but I won't judge—not my fellow Christ-followers, and certainly not those who haven't yet met Jesus.

I'm a long way from being able to make any of those claims, but the operative word in each one is "will." It's not a statement of self-determination;

unfortunately, personal pep talks accomplish very little permanent change. On my own, I won't see any of this come to fruition in my life.

But Jesus said, *"Follow Me… and I will make you fish for people!"* Good. Let's go.

Heavenly Father,

I want to consider all things as loss compared to the surpassing blessing of knowing You, except sometimes I don't really feel that. Usually because I'm distracted by a little toy or busy playing in the dirt.

I can be so childish when it comes to building my life in You, as You already know. That's why I take such joy in Your words: "Let the little children come to Me."

Thank You for Your limitless patience and restraint; Your kindness indeed leads me to repentance.

Never stop pushing me, even though I push back. Never stop chasing me, even though I hide. Help me learn to chase You in return. Lead me to maturity, that I might become that which You've intended me to be. Amen.

Afterword

It's a Wonderful Church

A re you still reading this? That's it! The book is over. No more baggage issues to write about. Time to close the book and put it down. Surely the Sunday morning service is about to start, so if you've been sitting here in the church library waiting, you can safely head into the sanctuary without having to stare at the Sunday School news board for another fifteen minutes, waiting to see if you recognize anyone out of the corner of your eye and want to talk to them. Make sure you put this book exactly where you found it on the library book shelf—you don't want to get the church librarian all wound up.

Maybe stop by the nursery on the way to the sanctuary. Undoubtedly, they're trying to get the kids to sit facing the same direction so they can show that cutesy video that teaches kids about the New Jerusalem with puppets and silly songs you can dance along to if you stay for a few minutes. "Coming, coming, coming down from heaven was the new, new, new golden city…" It looks like chaos now, but eight of these kids will one day take on leadership roles in this church and on their school campuses. At some point, your kids or grandkids might actually look up to them as someone who's really standing up for Jesus in the right ways.

Be sure to shake hands with the usher at the sanctuary doors. That guy has been a Sunday morning usher for thirty years and he's always got an extra bulletin for latecomers. His auto body repair business isn't doing too well, which is causing some stress around his retirement plans; he's also run into some health troubles lately, but he never misses a Sunday service and is always the last one to leave after stacking the chairs. Make sure you ask him about his health and if you can pray for him. Be sure you do it.

In heaven, you'll find out how he spent several sleepless nights, praying for your family when that tragedy hit a couple years ago.

Right about now, the youth pastor should be getting up to make the announcements about this Friday's youth event. Sounds like they're going to have some kind of game show where the kids have to eat disgusting stuff that will probably make a mess. It sure would be nice if some of those pierced-nosed kids would volunteer to help clean up... yeah, those same pierced-nosed kids who are being ostracized at school these days because they wrote an essay that made a public admission of being a Jesus-follower. Come to think of it, maybe it's not the end of the world if they don't do a great clean-up job this once. Maybe even consider complimenting that crazy blue hairstyle after the service.

Wow, the worship band is rocking today. That young guitar player is like God's Van Halen. Except he's standing still, his eyes closed because he's concentrating on offering his spiritual service of worship to God. As far as he's concerned, you folks in the congregation aren't even there and it's not a show. Some people in the audience might not appreciate his sizzling guitar riffs at the chorus, but I guarantee God's loving it.

Oh no, it's Missions Sunday today. Somehow you missed that in last week's bulletin. The pastor is up there now, interviewing a couple who left for some country that takes twenty-five hours of plane, bus, and canoe to get to. They've been working over there since 1982. Haven't they finished evangelizing that country yet? Apparently not, but they've set up a local online discipleship group to encourage the spiritual growth and fellowship of four churches that are somehow surviving without any trained leadership; recently the missionaries got a dial-up internet connection that lasts a couple hours per week. Not bad for folks who probably still have a VCR in their living room. Maybe you should increase your monthly contributions to a bit more than fifteen dollars...

You shake the pastor's hand on the way out afterwards. He looks a bit tired. Ever since he tried to counsel and intervene with that big family that's fighting, you've heard he's been up late dealing with painful phone calls. Oh yeah, and he's been taking it on the chin in emails ever since he delivered that sermon about Biblical giving and stewardship two weeks ago. Right from the opening moments, you could tell he was dreading the prospect of being mistaken for a salesman trying to separate people from their hard-earned cash. Sure, shake his hand, tell him you liked the service today—but better yet, invite him and his family over for dinner this week. Little do you know that he and his wife have been starting to question whether they have any true friends in the church.

Just before you head out to the parking lot, notice the new young couple standing awkwardly by the information table. That info table is a wealth of resources, isn't it? It's got all kinds of brochures, missionary profiles, concert announcements, event calendars, and free devotional books that look like they've been piled there since 1968. Lots of great stuff to read when you don't know anyone and have no one to talk to. Turns out this is a new mixed family visiting for the first time; later you'll learn that she and her first husband got divorced during a very stressful time when one of their kids was sick. They'd been going to a different church and their attendance dropped off during all the hospitalizations. After the divorce, her ex-husband left the church altogether and she remarried a father who was also divorced but had recently come to be a Christian. Turns out they were asked to leave that former church on account of their present "adultery." Maybe you can invite the mom to bring her kids to your church's midweek kids' program, where both the kids and the mom eventually make a few nonjudgmental friends who are just happy they've come. Five years from now, that lady finds healing, forgiveness, and a new life in Christ. At her baptism, the church family wipes away tears to hear her testimony of God's powerful regeneration and old things becoming new. Later, she hosts a weekly meeting in the library for people seeking God's healing and restoration after divorce.

On the way out the door, you brush against a guy you haven't seen in a while. His wife manages to drag him to church every now and then. It must be a bit early for the start of fishing season, otherwise there's no way he'd be here. As it is, the expression on his face makes him look like a middle-aged guy who's stuck following his wife through the aisles of bras and white underwear at Sears. He just wants to get outta there! He's been hanging around church for years, but it's patently obviously he's got no interest. You've even heard a couple stories of work shenanigans in the past that make you feel sorry for his wife. The guy's clearly had lots of chances to come to Christ, but his body language is shouting, "No way!" Say hi anyway. Ask if he's ready for fishing season to start. Ask about his new boat and maybe offer to join him sometime. Even if it's a Sunday morning. One day in heaven, you'll be stunned to see him come over and shake your hand. "God eventually got a hold of me," he'll say. "It's a good thing you were nice to me that Sunday, otherwise it would have been my last." Even more amazing: the guy's got a huge family up there with him in heaven—his wife, kids, and their kids were rocked when he gave his life to Christ at the age of seventy-nine, three years before he died but with plenty of time to make amends with all his estranged children who wandered away from the church themselves until they saw a supernatural transformation in an old, angry man.

The church can be a frustrating place. Hollow, fake, business-like, country club, all kinds of dysfunctional gatherings. Or it can be a beautiful place, full of terribly imperfect people who somehow soldier on, despite variable baggage, to create a community characterized by Christ-directed reconciliation. As the baggage drops, the brighter the light of the church gets and the more attractive it becomes to the world outside.

Well, that's it. This book is really finished. But that's just it: this book is nothing more than words on a page. Words by themselves do nothing. Time to put down the book, drop the baggage, join your fellow Christ-followers, and go to church.

Wait, I'm coming with you.